Also by Jon Paulien

Armageddon at the Door

The Day That Changed the World

The Deep Things of God:
An Insider's Guide to the Book of Revelation

The Gospel From Patmos

Everlasting Gospel, Ever-changing World

What the Bible Says About the End-time

Jon Paulien

Seven Keys

Unlocking the Secrets of Revelation

Pacific Press®
Publishing Association

Nampa, Idaho | www.pacificpress.com

Cover design by Steve Lanto
Cover design resources from Dreamstime.com
Inside design by Aaron Troia

The author assumes full responsibility for the accuracy of all facts and quotations as cited in this book.

Unless otherwise noted, all scriptures are the author's translation.

Scripture quotations marked NIV are from the HOLY BIBLE, NEW INTERNA-TIONAL VERSION®. Copyright © 1973, 1978, 1984 by International Bible Society. Used by permission of Zondervan Publishing House. All rights reserved.

Scriptures marked KJV are from the King James Version.

You can obtain additional copies of this book by calling toll-free 1-800-765-6955 or by visiting www.adventistbookcenter.com.

Library of Congress Cataloging-in-Publication Data:

Paulien, Jon, 1949-
Seven keys : unlocking the secrets of Revelation / by Jon Paulien.
  p. cm.
ISBN 978-0-8163-2373-9 (pbk.)
1. Bible. N. T. Revelation—Criticism, interpretation, etc. I. Title.
BS2825.52.P39 2009
228'.06—dc22

                                                        2009042719

August 2021

Dedication

To Wil Alexander,
a "living legend,"
mentor, and friend

Table of Contents

Seven Keys · *Part One*

Chapter One

As We Begin

THE FIRST eight verses of the book of Revelation serve as its introduction; in them the author, the apostle John, tells us how we are to interpret this prophetic book. I can think of no better starting point for us when we're considering how we should understand the book today. So, let's start at the beginning, Revelation 1:1–8:

> The revelation of Jesus Christ, which God gave to Him to show to His servants what must happen soon. And He signified it, sending it through His angel to His servant John, who testified concerning the Word of God and the testimony of Jesus Christ, which he saw. Blessed is the one who reads and those which hear the words of this prophecy, and keep the things which are written in it, for the time is near.
>
> John, to the seven churches which are in Asia:

Grace to you and peace from the One who is, and who was, and who is to come, and from the seven spirits which are before His throne, and from Jesus Christ, the faithful witness, the firstborn of the dead, and the Ruler of the kings of the earth. To the One who loves us, and has freed us from our sins by His blood, and has made us a kingdom, priests before God, even His Father—to Him be glory and power forever and ever. Amen.

Behold, He is coming with the clouds, and every eye will see Him, including those who pierced Him, and all tribes of the earth will mourn over Him. Yes, amen. "I am the Alpha and the Omega," says the Lord God, "the One who is and who was and who is to come, the Almighty."

What can we learn from the author's introduction? First, look at verse 4: "John, to the seven churches, which are in Asia." Right here at the beginning, John tells us plainly that when he wrote the book of Revelation, he was addressing seven specific churches in Asia.

Asia was a Roman province in the western part of what is the country of Turkey today. In the first century, there were several Christian churches in Roman Asia, and it was to these churches that John was writing. While we are often tempted to read the book of Revelation as if it were written solely to us, this text tells us that in actuality, it was written two thousand years ago to real people who lived in a real place. In fact, this is stated not only in the introduction of the book, but also in the last chapter (verse 16). So, we can conclude that the entire book was sent to those churches.

Because the entire book was written to a specific context in the ancient world, many scholars promote a theory called *preterism*. This interpretive approach says that Revelation isn't a prophecy of events that would take place long after it was written. Rather, the book's meaning is limited to the people of its time and place—the Christians who lived in Asia Minor two thousand years ago.

There's an element of truth in this. The book of Revelation was definitely written to people of its time and place. It definitely meant something to them, and the more we can learn about what they understood it to mean, the better our understanding of the book will be. But preterism calls us to read the book in too limited a way. God's intention for Revelation wasn't limited to the time and place of the seven churches of Roman Asia. It was bigger than that.

John's introduction to the book points to this larger

purpose. Verse 7 of the first chapter says, "Behold He is coming with the clouds, and every eye will see Him, including those who pierced Him, and all the tribes of the earth will mourn over Him. Yes, amen." So, the book of Revelation addresses the very end of time and events related to that time, such as the second coming of Jesus.

Of course, many people search Revelation for references to current events. Is September 11 in there? Does it say anything about the war on terror—or even Barack Obama?

Since it is clear that parts of the book of Revelation focus on the end times, on *our* future, some people have come up with an approach to interpreting the book called *futurism.* They attempt to read Revelation as if the whole book speaks directly to the end of time and to no other time in history.

Again, there is an element of truth here. The book of Revelation *does* speak to the end of time. It *does* speak to our future, and we need to take those parts of Revelation seriously. But we have already seen that it speaks to ancient times as well. So the futurist approach by itself is no more adequate than is the preterist approach.

There is a third way of understanding the book of Revelation. John's introduction to his book points toward this one, too, in verse 3 of that opening passage. It says,

"Blessed is the one who reads and those who hear the words of this prophecy."

In *Koine* Greek, the language in which John wrote Revelation, the word translated "hearing" has a special grammatical function. It can mean hearing *with* understanding or hearing *without* understanding, depending on the grammatical case of the object. The case used in verse 3 indicates that John expects that those who hear someone read the book of Revelation will hear it *with understanding*. In other words, he expects that whoever reads this book and whoever hears someone read it aloud will understand it. John didn't write Revelation just for people living in the first century, and he didn't write it just for those living at the time of the end of the world. Rather, it was meant to be understood *throughout* history. God intended that anyone at any time who picks up this book and reads it will understand the basic message it contains.

From observations like this, some readers of Revelation have developed the idea that anybody at any time can benefit from the book, and there is certainly truth in that. But some people have taken this notion a bit further and have come up with an idea called *idealism.* They say, "The book of Revelation isn't really written to the first century, and it's not really a prophecy of things at the end of time either. It's a symbolic way of presenting broad, general principles for Christians to live by." In other words, anybody can read this book and draw from it general principles for life.

Again, there is an element of truth here: blessed is everyone who reads and everyone who hears the words of the book. But the suggestion that Revelation contains only general principles for living doesn't adequately take into account the full realities of the book.

Summing up what we've considered so far: There are three popular approaches to the book of Revelation. There's preterism, which is particularly popular with secular scholars of the book. It says Revelation spoke only about first-century events. There's futurism, which says the book speaks only about the end of time. And third, there is idealism, which says Revelation presents only broad, general principles of Christian living.

Another way

I believe, however, that if you take the entire introduction of Revelation seriously, there's an even better method for studying the book. It's called *historicism*. It takes the first-century standpoint of preterism, the future standpoint of futurism, and the general interests of idealism as aspects of the book's purpose, but it doesn't limit our understanding to any of those approaches. Instead, it takes all the evidence of Revelation seriously. It says that readers should realize that some aspects of the book speak to the beginning of the Christian era. For instance, the introductory passage, in verses 1–8, sets the stage in the first century. But this method also notes that other aspects of Revelation focus on the end of time, and that still others are of general value in every time and place. Historicism, rightly understood, is the best method because it allows each text to locate itself in time; it doesn't limit the meaning in an arbitrary way as the other approaches do. It tells us that the book applies to the beginning of the Christian era, to the end of the Christian era, and to all the time between those two points.

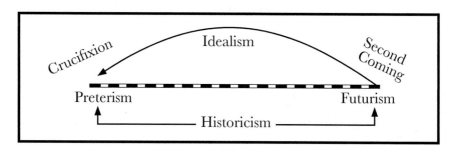

How then should historicism be applied in practice? John gives us a hint right in the first verse. He tells us there exactly how historicism works. In verse 1, he speaks of the things that "must happen soon." One of the things we'll discover about the book of Revelation is that John often points the reader to earlier literature, particularly the Old Testament. He uses a word or a phrase that points to an earlier text. For instance, the phrase we just noted in verse 1 is pretty rare in the Bible. In fact, it occurs in only three places in the Bible. It appears here in verse 1 but also in Daniel 2:28 (in the Greek translation of the Old Testament called the Septuagint), which tells us that Daniel showed King Nebuchadnezzar what *"must happen* in the last days" (emphasis added).

Perhaps you remember the story. In chapter 2, the prophet Daniel interprets for King Nebuchadnezzar his famous dream. The king had dreamed of a statue made of four metals: gold, silver, bronze, and iron. The statue represents a sequence of nations in the course of history, each nation symbolized by a different metal. The text (verse 45) says that the dream has shown to the king what will be in the last days.

In essence, Daniel tells Nebuchadnezzar, "You are the head of gold. Another nation is going to come after you; that nation will be inferior to you just as silver is inferior to gold. Next, a third nation, represented by the bronze portion of the statue, will dominate; then a fourth nation, iron; and finally, at the end of time, the kingdom of God will come."

So, the prophecy in chapter 2 pictures a sequence of events running from Daniel's day all the way to the end of time. Scholars call the literature containing prophecies like this *apocalyptic*. Apocalyptic literature commonly uses a sequence of symbols to portray sequences of historical events.

How does Daniel 2 help us understand Revelation? Here's where it becomes interesting. Right at the beginning of the first verse of Revelation, John alludes to Daniel 2 when he says that in what follows, he's going to describe things that "must happen soon." The words "must happen" recall the "must happen" in Daniel 2. Revelation follows that phrase with the word "soon." What follows that phrase in Daniel? The words "in the last days."

- Revelation 1:1—"must happen *soon*"
- Daniel 2:45—"must happen *in the last days*"

Daniel wrote about six hundred years before the time of John. Daniel was looking at the whole sequence of events that leads up to the end of time. By picking up Daniel's language, John is saying something to this effect: "Revelation is going to be unpacking the book of Daniel as well as other Old Testament books. It will follow the same approach that God used when He spoke to Daniel. In the book of Revelation, you are going to find sequences of symbols that point to sequences of events that haven't happened yet."

(Relax! We won't be getting into a lot of that history. We're simply trying to understand the basics of Revelation— how it is composed, what we should expect.)

In other words, the book of Revelation is a lot like Daniel 2. In Revelation, just as in the book of Daniel, we find prophecies of sequential events. As in Daniel, these historical sequences run from the prophet's day all the way to the end of time—in Revelation, then, from John's day, the first century after Christ, all the way to the Second Coming and even beyond. And in both books there is a consistent symbolism—except Revelation doesn't have a statue made up of various metals. Instead, Revelation pictures a sequence of animals—some really strange animals, kinds you won't see in a zoo.

Before we get into that, though, we need to find some specific answers to the question, How do we interpret Revelation? As the title of this book suggests, we're going to use seven keys to unlock the prophecies of Revelation. Many of these keys can also be found in Revelation's introduction, chapter 1, verses 1–8. We will discover others by noting the characteristics of the entire book.

Chapter Two

The Seven Keys

THERE ARE seven keys that enable us to interpret Revelation consistently and accurately. When we use them, we can find God's will and understand His plan and what He asks of us as He works it out. Let's take a look at these keys.

Key #1: A divine revelation

The first of these keys to interpreting Revelation is understanding that this biblical book is a divine revelation—its content came to John directly from God. We call it the book of Revelation because it is a revelation from God.

Revelation 1:1–3 explicitly makes this claim. It says this book is "the revelation of Jesus Christ, which God gave to Him to show to His servants what must happen soon. And He signified it, sending it through His angel to His servant John, who testified concerning the Word of God and the testimony of Jesus Christ, which he saw.

Blessed is the one who reads and those who hear the words of this prophecy and keep the things which are written in it, for the time is near."

John doesn't say, "Well, some stuff occurred to me, and I thought maybe I'd write you a book and tell you what I've been thinking." No, John tells us that the symbols in this book aren't his own idea. He didn't make these visions up. They are based on the revelation of Jesus Christ that God gave him. God sent this revelation to John through Jesus Christ and through an angel. And when John received this message from God in vision, he wrote it down for people to read. So this passage describes a chain of revelation that starts with God and ends in the form of this book that we're studying.

In other words, when the "revelation of Jesus Christ" comes down to John, he sees it as the "testimony of Jesus Christ." Then he writes out what he has seen and calls it "the words of this prophecy." There's a chain of events here, one building on the other. The book of Revelation reflects what John received from Jesus. And what John sees reflects something that happened between God the Father and Jesus. They worked together on this project just as They were working together before time began.

So the book of Revelation is a divine revelation. This is extremely important for us because it tells us that this is a genuine, trustworthy picture of the future. I could tell you what I *think* is going to happen in five years, or ten years, or a hundred years, or even a thousand years. I could tell you what I think, but I don't *know* what will happen in the future. I sometimes try to project certain political events or certain trends that I see happening in society, and I'm not too bad at doing that. I sometimes get the immediate trends right. But for the most part, I don't have a clue what will happen ten years from now or a hundred years from now. So if I were to write a book of prophecy for you—*Jon Paulien's Prophecies*—you wouldn't pay much attention. And I wouldn't expect you to because it would be just my ideas, just my guesses.

But if the book of Revelation comes from God, if it's a book of God's own vision of the future, then it's something solid, something dependable. The book of Revelation is worth studying because it is a *divine* revelation. It's worth studying because what it says about the future is true and we can count on its prophecies happening just as God has said they would. Reading the book of Revelation as a prophecy of the future would be pointless if it weren't a divine revelation.

Of the four approaches to Revelation that I mentioned in the previous chapter, both futurism and historicism are grounded in the conviction that God is speaking to us in this book—that its prophecies are real and that they are important for our lives now and for as long as time will last.

Key #2: *The Old Testament*

The second key to interpretation is the Old Testament. Revelation is the last book of the Bible, the last part of the New Testament. So, in a sense, it's the climax of the Bible. But that isn't all. Revelation deliberately alludes to all kinds of Old Testament passages—it contains bits of language from nearly every part of the Old Testament. Biblical scholar William Milligan wrote, "The book [of Revelation] is absolutely steeped in the memories, the incidents, the thoughts, and the language of the Church's past. To such an extent is this the case that it may be doubted whether it contains a single figure not drawn from the Old Testament, or a single complete sentence not more or less built up of materials brought from the same."[1]

In the preceding chapter we saw an example of John's use of the Old Testament in the first verse of the book, which alludes to Daniel 2. Revelation 1:7, which is also part of the introductory passage, contains another example. This verse says, "Behold, He is coming with the clouds, and every eye will see Him, including those who pierced Him, and all tribes of the earth will mourn over Him. Yes, amen."

Who is this verse talking about? It is talking about Jesus, the One who brings the vision to John. According to this text, when Jesus comes every eye will see Him. In other words, the whole world will see Him. His coming is a universal event. Everyone will see Him, and all the tribes of the earth, all the peoples of the earth, will mourn for Him.

What's the point? John has chosen to use wording in this text that reminds us of an Old Testament text. He wants us to refer to that earlier text in order to understand what he's describing in Revelation.

The passage John has drawn from here is Zechariah 12:10–12: "And I will pour out on the house of David and the inhabitants of Jerusalem a spirit of grace and supplication. They will look on me, the one they have pierced, and they will mourn for him as one mourns for an only child, and grieve bitterly for him, as one grieves for a firstborn son. On that day the weeping in Jerusalem will be great. . . . The land will mourn, each clan by itself" (NIV).

Who is speaking in Zechariah 12? Not Jesus. Rather, it is the God of the Old Testament. So the God of the

Old Testament is actually taking on a human aspect here. That is why many New Testament writers saw a foreshadowing of Jesus in the behavior of the Old Testament God as portrayed by this text. In this text God says, "They will look on me, the one they have pierced." But then the text switches from first person to third: "They will mourn for *him*." Here in the Old Testament, then, there is the sense that the Members of the Godhead have taken on different roles. That's why New Testament writers saw in this text a hint of the work of Jesus. That's why in writing the book of Revelation, John took this text about the Old Testament God and applied it to Jesus.

The text in Zechariah, then, is spiritualized. It refers to the One who walked among us in human flesh—the One who lived in Palestine in the first century. He is the One who was pierced. He is the One this text is prophesying about.

Notice also what else happens in Zechariah 12. This passage says that it is the inhabitants of Jerusalem and tribes who live on the land around Jerusalem who see Him, who mourn for Him.

So, in Zechariah, it is God who comes. In Zechariah, it is God who is pierced. In Zechariah, the clans of Jerusalem mourn. In Zechariah, Jerusalem itself mourns. Zechariah 12, then, localizes the actions of God geographically. What He does occurs in relation to the people who live in Jerusalem and the surrounding area.

In contrast, in Revelation 1 there is a shifting—a spiritualizing—of the God-concept of Zechariah 12. In Revelation 1, it is Jesus who comes. It is Jesus who is pierced. And it's the tribes of the whole earth and the earth itself who mourn, not just the city of Jerusalem and the tribes around that city.

Zechariah 12	Revelation 1:7
God comes	Jesus comes
God is pierced	Jesus is pierced
Clans of Jerusalem	Tribes of the earth
Jerusalem mourns	The earth mourns

You can see what is happening. Revelation takes the things the Old Testament applied locally and makes them worldwide. It takes the divine things of the Old Testament and applies them spiritually to Jesus Christ. So the book of Revelation universalizes and Christianizes the Old Testament.

Remember the famous Left Behind™ series of books and movies?[2] It's a very interesting series, and those who have written for that project are people of faith. I have great respect for them. But I have a problem with the way that they understand Revelation. They see every-thing in Revelation as local. When they see "Jerusalem" in Revelation, they think the book is referring to literal Jerusalem. When they see "Euphrates," it's simply a river in the Middle East. In fact, in their view, everything in Revelation is about the Middle East. It's all about *politics* at the end of time. Yet Revelation interacts with the Old Testament by spiritualizing these things. It applies them universally. It applies them to everyone living in the Christian age. Revelation is a book about how everything works out in Jesus Christ.

Let's look now at another aspect of the way Revelation relates to the Old Testament. The writers of the New Testament use the Old Testament in four ways. First, New Testament writers *cite* the Old Testament. This use is something like making a footnote. The writers quote Old Testament language and give a reference to the book the quotation came from.

Second, New Testament writers *quote* the Old Testament. They quote enough of a passage to make it clear to the reader where the quotation came from. For example, if I were to quote the national anthem of the United States, any American would recognize immediately where I got it from. Or if I were to say, "Mary had a little lamb, its fleece was white as snow," most people would know that those lines come from a familiar children's poem.

Third, New Testament writers *allude to* the Old Testament. In an allusion, the writer takes a word or phrase and expects the readers to know what he is talking about. For instance, in most of the world today I could say just the name "Obama" and everyone would know what and who I was talking about. An allusion points the reader to a specific, larger context. In the case of Revelation, that familiar context is the Old Testament.

Fourth, New Testament writers *echo* the Old Testament. In an echo, the writer takes language that sounds like it's coming from an earlier piece of literature, but uses that language for a different purpose than the original writer had when he wrote the words. The second writer isn't thinking about how the language was used or what it meant in the original literature; the second writer uses the term or phrase entirely for his own purpose, certain that readers will understand it in its own right.

Now here's the interesting thing. In the book of Revelation, there are no citations of the Old Testament and no quotations. There are only allusions and echoes. In other words, the author of Revelation pulls in an Old Testament word here, a phrase there, and the barest hint somewhere else. So, to truly understand the book of Revelation, we need to know the Old Testament thoroughly. If we want to understand fully John's intention, we need to be prepared to recognize mere words and phrases.

Perhaps this leaves you saying, "Oh, my knowledge of the Old Testament is so limited. I'll never understand Revelation."

Don't worry—the more you read, the more you'll learn. You'll see how much fun studying Revelation is if you give it a try. Studying Revelation is a lot like playing a Nintendo game—it's full of puzzles you have to solve. You work it here, and you work it there, and finally you figure your way through. And what's your reward when you solve the puzzle? You get to move to a tougher level! The book of Revelation is like that. Just when you think you're beginning to understand it, you get to move to another level, and you realize, "Oops, maybe I didn't understand as much as I thought I did." It's true that when it comes to Revelation's use of the Old Testament, there's a lot to learn. But learning it is very exciting.

The fact that Revelation is so deep should teach us to avoid becoming too dogmatic about our understanding of the book. When we learn a few things, it's easy for us to say, "I know what I'm talking about." But I've studied the book of Revelation for thirty years, and there are many things about it that I still don't understand. And I have to admit there are many things that God will let other people discover. Or maybe some of those puzzles will never be fully understood, at least in this life. Maybe God put some of those puzzles in there to keep us searching, to keep us learning, to keep us growing.

Key #3: The New Testament

The third key for interpreting the book of Revelation is the New Testament. We've seen that Revelation uses the Old Testament extensively by allusion and echo. But Revelation is a New Testament book. It's a Christian book. It's the revelation of Jesus Christ. He is present everywhere in the book. As you work your way through the book, you'll realize that there are lots of connections to the gospel, the Cross, Christian churches, and more.

At times, the language may differ from that of the rest of the New Testament. It may be Old Testament language. But there's a harmony of ideas between Revelation and the New Testament. The theology of Revelation doesn't differ from the theology of the Gospels and the theology of Paul. Revelation has its own unique emphases, but there is an underlining harmony with the rest of the New Testament. In fact, one of my favorite authors wrote, "In [the book of] Revelation all the books of the Bible meet and end."[3] In other words, the book of

Revelation is kind of like the finale to the biblical symphony. Like the last act of a play. In the book of Revelation, the Old Testament and the New Testament—all the sixty-five other books of the Bible—come together. The better you understand the rest of the Bible, the better you'll understand Revelation.

For this reason, one of the most dangerous things you can do is study the book of Revelation by itself. People have died because of strange interpretations of the book of Revelation. People have started wars and pursued all kinds of political aims based on the book of Revelation. David Koresh gives us an example of the potential destructiveness that faulty interpretations of the book of Revelation can produce. If you're not reading the book of Revelation in its own context, following up its allusions to the entire Bible, it's easy to misunderstand the book. It's easy to take it places where God wouldn't want you to go.

The book of Revelation is a New Testament book. The essential message of the book doesn't contradict the gospel of Jesus Christ.

Key #4: A symbolic book

Now we come to a fourth key to interpretation: the book of Revelation is symbolic. The very first verse makes that clear: "The revelation of Jesus Christ, which God gave to Him to show to His servants what must happen soon. *And He signified it,* sending it through His angel to His servant John."

Notice the italicized part of that text: "He signified it." The Greek word translated "signified" is a very special word. It tells us that this is a symbolic book, a symbolic representation of future events.

As we noted earlier with reference to the Left Behind series, the language of Revelation is not to be taken literally most of the time. Revelation is a symbolic book; it is filled with symbols. And it is God who chose those symbols. That's an extremely important point. Through symbolic visions, God is showing us the message He wants to communicate. If you understand the symbols, you'll understand the message. If you don't understand the symbols, you won't get the message.

I noted earlier that there are animals in Revelation. For instance, it describes a seven-headed dragon with ten horns. The dragon is lurking near a woman, who is standing on the moon, all shiny and sparkly. You probably haven't experienced anything like that dragon in real life. If you were walking in the forest and you saw a seven-headed dragon, what would you know? You'd know you'd been drinking! You'd know that because there's no such thing as a seven-headed dragon, and you probably haven't ever seen a woman standing on the moon either. The book of Revelation contains creatures that are unique; they're different than anything we've seen in nature.

The book of Revelation is a symbolic book. If you take it literally, as our friends who wrote the Left Behind books do, you're going to misunderstand it. Revelation is designed to symbolize the truth that God had in mind for us to understand. So we must be careful not to take things in the book of Revelation too literally.

Are there occasions where the book can be taken literally? Sure. If interpreting something in Revelation as a symbol makes no sense at all, then don't interpret it that way. For example, when Revelation speaks of Jesus Christ, is this Jesus Christ a symbol? I don't think so. It's simply a personal name of Someone the writer of Revelation knew well and whom we know through the New Testament. So Jesus Christ is an example of something in Revelation that is clearly literal.

But in the book of Revelation, the normal run of language is symbolic. You should take the language of Revelation symbolically, unless it becomes clear that a literal reading is required.

Key #5: Asia Minor setting

A fifth key to interpreting Revelation is the setting to which the first verses of the book refer. John wrote this book on the Isle of Patmos near Asia Minor. He sent it to seven churches that were also in Asia Minor. And in Scripture—as elsewhere—God always meets people where they are. That is the way He has always worked.

In Daniel 2, God gives a pagan king a symbolic vision about four successive earthly kingdoms followed by the kingdom of God. How does God bring this message to the pagan king? In the form of an idol—something the king would understand. Notice that when, five chapters later, God gives Daniel a vision about the same four earthly kingdoms followed by God's kingdom, He gives him a picture of creation: a stormy sea, animals, and a Son of man who has dominion over the animals. The message in both visions is the same: four kingdoms are followed by the kingdom of God. But God shapes the message to meet the differing minds of a pagan king and a Hebrew prophet. God meets people where they are.

Why are there four Gospels in the New Testament when one Gospel could tell the basic story of Jesus? Because there are many different types of people. Four Gospels tell the story of Jesus more completely than just one would. Perhaps Matthew is your favorite, but someone else likes Mark. I prefer John. Each Gospel meets a different type of mind or personality. Through these four pictures of Jesus, we all can get a clearer understanding of Him. God meets people where they are.

This principle is at work also in the seven churches of Revelation. Each gets a different picture of Jesus; each sees and understands God a little bit differently. God meets people where they are. He approaches each church in a unique way.

When we go really deep into the book of Revelation, we discover that there are live symbols in the book. These are symbols that come right out of the culture in which John lived. David Aune wrote the largest commentary ever on the book of Revelation. He points out that the picture of Jesus in chapter 1, verses 13–18, seems an awful lot like that of Hekate, the most important goddess in Asia Minor.[4] Her worshipers considered her to be the mistress of the cosmos, of the universe.

Among other things, Hekate was called the first and the last, the beginning and the end. She was the goddess of revelation. She had the keys of heaven and hell. She would travel up to heaven, and travel down to hell, and then she would return to earth and explain what was going on in those places.

Amazingly, Jesus is described in the same terms in Revelation 1!

Why would an inspired writer compare Jesus to a pagan goddess? I can suggest at least two reasons. First, to communicate well to pagans, John had to use their language. And second, and more specifically, to refute what the pagans believed, John had to use their language. So, in describing Jesus, John used language that brought Hekate to the ancient reader's mind.

What's the point? Something like the following: "You will find the things that you seek from this goddess only if you come to Jesus. Hekate isn't the answer to the problems of the world. Jesus can bring you everything that you hope to find in her."

That's what a live symbol is all about. The book of Revelation took symbols right out of the ancient context and used them to speak powerfully to its time. The more we understand that ancient context, the more we can understand what John would tell us today. Everyone who reads Revelation and everyone who hears it read is intended to understand these important things.

Key #6: An ancient apocalypse

A sixth key to interpreting Revelation correctly is our

recognition that it is an ancient apocalypse. *Apocalypse* is a genre, a style of literature. Apocalyptic literature uses symbols, such as strange animals and so forth.

Why does the book of Revelation use such strange language? Why be so difficult, so symbolic, so out of tune with our culture today?

The reality is that we are familiar with apocalyptic. It is a part of today's world too. Have you ever heard of *The Lion King*? It was the most popular animated feature film ever made. Is *The Lion King* an animal story? Yes, it has lions and hyenas and antelopes and so forth—various kinds of African animals. But is *The Lion King* really an animal story? If you've seen it, you know the answer. *The Lion King* isn't really about animals. It's actually an apocalypse. It tells a story about a perfect world that was ruined and how a son of the "king" comes back and restores the perfect world that was lost. It's an apocalypse. The animals don't really represent animals. They're symbols of people. They're symbols of ideas. They're symbols of political interactions. *The Lion King*, like Revelation, is an apocalypse.

Apocalyptic teaches us things that we might not easily learn some other way. So you see, the apocalyptic genre isn't totally foreign to today's world. The strange animals of Revelation are symbols we can understand in a general way.

In the ancient world, there were two types of apocalyptic. There was historical apocalyptic, which featured a sequence of events symbolized by animals or metals or various other symbols. The key idea of historical apocalyptic was the sequence of historical events.

The other type of apocalyptic is mystical apocalyptic. It features journeys to heaven and to hell. Perhaps you've heard of Dante. His work, *Divine Comedy,* provides a good example of mystical apocalyptic.

Revelation contains both types of apocalyptic. It has historical sequences such as that pictured by the seven trumpets. And it has journeys up to heaven—see, for instance, chapters 4 and 5. Some of these journeys even take readers to the end of time.

However, while apocalyptic comprises a major part of Revelation, this book isn't all apocalyptic. It also contains songs, prayers, and letters. So Revelation is what I call a "mixed genre." Consequently, we need to take into account the nature of the part of the book we're reading or studying.

Key #7: Chiastic structure

The seventh key to the interpretation of Revelation is chiastic structure. A chiastic structure is like an inverted

V—some call it a pyramid structure. Books arranged or sequenced in a chiastic structure have their climax—their most important point—in the middle. In our culture, most books build toward a climax at or near the end. That wasn't necessarily true of ancient books—particularly books influenced by Hebrew thought patterns and forms.

Let's look at some evidence. Revelation 1:1–3, the beginning of the book, says that Jesus sent the revelation through His angel. Chapter 22, verses 6–10, part of the book's conclusion, repeats that thought: "He sent His angel." Both passages contain the phrases "to show to His servants" and "what must happen soon." "Blessed" appears in both places. Chapter 22's "keep the prophecy of the book" parallels chapter 1's use of "the words of this prophecy." And both passages say "the time is near." In other words, these two passages, one at the beginning of the book and one at its end, seem to be saying virtually the same thing.

Revelation 1:1–3	**Revelation 22:6–10**
"Sent through His angel"	"Sent His angel"
"To show to His servants"	"To show to His servants"
"What must happen soon"	"What must happen soon"

"Blessed"	"Blessed"
"The words of this prophecy"	"The words of this book"
"For the time is near"	"For the time is near"

Revelation contains numerous connections like these, in which parallels occur in stair-step fashion up and down a literary pyramid. The seven churches in chapters 2 and 3 parallel the New Jerusalem of chapters 21 and 22. The seals of chapters 4 to 7 parallel chapters 19 and 20. The trumpets of chapter 9 parallel the plagues of chapter 16. The whole thing ends up looking something like this:

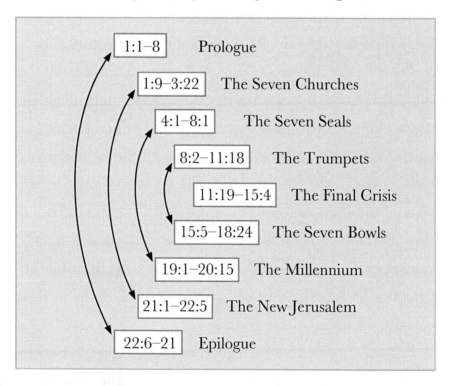

1:1–8   Prologue

1:9–3:22   The Seven Churches

4:1–8:1   The Seven Seals

8:2–11:18   The Trumpets

11:19–15:4   The Final Crisis

15:5–18:24   The Seven Bowls

19:1–20:15   The Millennium

21:1–22:5   The New Jerusalem

22:6–21   Epilogue

What you see from this diagram is a visual portrayal of the structure of the book of Revelation. There are nine parts to the book: a prologue, an epilogue, and seven major sections. As we've already seen, there are threads that tie these parts together—the prologue parallels the epilogue, the seven churches parallel the New Jerusalem, and so on all the way to the top. It's a pyramid structure—a chiasm.

Here's the point. As I said above, in chiastic Hebrew thinking, the main point doesn't come at the end. It stands in the middle. In other words, the key events of the book are the events that take place right at its heart. And the heart of the book of Revelation is found in chapters 12 to 14, which describe the final crisis of earth's history.

I wasn't the first to see this. A Roman Catholic scholar named Elizabeth Fiorenza developed a similar idea. She has a chiastic or pyramid structure like mine.[5] (We came to the idea independently.) But she takes the concept a step further. She says the crucial center of this central part of the book is found in chapter 14: it's the introduction of the 144,000 in verses 1–5 and the three angels' messages of verses 6–12.[6] I disagree with Roman Catholics on many things, but when a Roman Catholic scholar is right, I'm happy to agree!

So, yes, I agree that the center of the book is in chapters 12–14. And I agree that the center of the center is in chapter 14, particularly the three angels' messages in verses 6–12. But I take it one step further yet. I believe there is a center of the center of the center in the book of Revelation. I believe that ultimate center is found in chapter 14, verse 7. The last part of verse 7 says, "Worship Him who made the heaven, and the earth, and the sea, and the fountains of water." That to me is the heart of the chiasm. That is the climax of the climax of the climax. The book of Revelation is a call to worship Him who made the heaven and earth, the sea, and the fountains of waters.

And guess what! That idea comes from the Old Testament. It comes from Exodus 20:11, in the fourth commandment. As we approach the end of time, the heart of the book of Revelation calls us to worship God in the way that God has asked us to worship Him, and that includes worship on the Sabbath day. Understanding the structure of the book of Revelation gives us the key to its central message.

When we explore Revelation using the keys it has given us, we'll discover much that piques our interest and that also gives us direction as to how we are to live. Understanding Revelation is certainly worth our best effort.

---

1. William Milligan, *The Revelation of St. John* (London: Macmillan and Co., 1886), 72.

2. Trademark owned by Tyndale House Publishers, Wheaton, Illinois.

3. Ellen G. White, *The Acts of the Apostles* (Mountain View, Calif.: Pacific Press® Publishing Association, 1911), 585.

4. David E. Aune, *Revelation 1–5,* Anchor Bible, vol. 52A (Dallas: Word Books, 1997), 104.

5. Elisabeth Schüssler Fiorenza, *The Book of Revelation: Justice and Judgment* (Philadelphia: Fortress Press, 1985), 170–177.

6. Ibid., 188, 189.

Seven Keys • *Part Two*

Chapter Three

On the Island of Patmos

W E BEGIN part 2 by looking at the seven churches. The introduction to the letters sent to the seven churches comes just after the first eight verses of Revelation, which we looked at in part 1. Now we come to the verses that immediately follow that introduction, verses 9–11. "I, John, your brother and companion in the affliction and kingdom and patient endurance which is in Jesus, came to be on the island which is called Patmos, on account of the Word of God and the testimony of Jesus. I was in the Spirit during the Lord's Day, and I heard a loud voice like a trumpet behind me. 'Write what you see in a book and send it to the seven churches, to Ephesus, Smyrna, Pergamos, Thyatira, Sardis, Philadelphia and Laodicea.' "

Here John names the cities where the seven churches were located. Notice that this text says that John sees a vision and then is told to "Write what you see." He is told to write down the vision he is receiving and send it to the churches. The text also tells us that John is on the island of Patmos on account of the Word of God and the testimony of Jesus. Just exactly what this means isn't clear. How could the Word of God or the testimony of Jesus put John on an island?

Many ancient traditions say that John was on the island as a punishment for his Christian faith—that because of his Christian beliefs, the Roman authorities exiled him to Patmos. This island, which is about six miles long and three miles across at its widest point, lies just off the coast of Asia Minor, twenty or thirty miles into the Aegean Sea.

So, John was exiled from the seven churches with which he had been working. While on Patmos, he had a vision and then was asked to write down what he saw and send the message to those seven churches.

Jesus and the seven churches

What does John see that he's told to write out and send to the churches?

And in the midst of the lampstands was One like a Son of man, dressed in a foot-length robe and wrapped around the chest with a golden sash. His

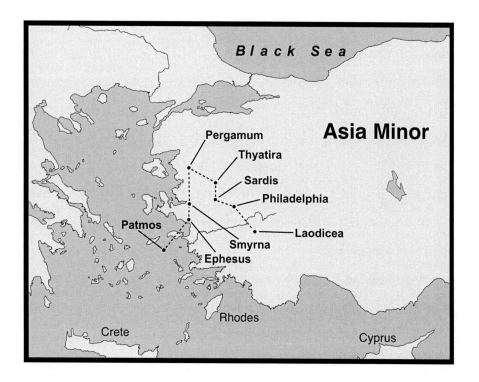

head and His hairs were white like wool, white as snow; and His eyes were like a flame of fire. His feet were like polished brass which had been purified in a furnace, and His voice was like the sound of many waters. He had seven stars in His right hand, a sharp, two-edged sword was coming out of His mouth, and His face was like the sun shining in its strength (Revelation 1:13–16).

These verses give us a magnificent picture of Jesus. They tell us more than a dozen of His characteristics.

And here's something interesting: as Jesus is introduced to each church, only two or three of these characteristics are mentioned. He's introduced to the first church as the One who holds the seven stars and stands among the lampstands (2:1). He's introduced to the second church as the First and the Last, the One who died and who came to life (verse 8). To the third church He is the One with the sharp, double-edged sword coming out of His mouth (verse 12).

Notice that Jesus presents Himself to each church in a completely unique way. He respects their differences. He meets their unique needs—or, as I said earlier, He meets each church where it is. This is one of the strongest interpretive principles for the study of the Bible. The message is from God, but the vehicle of the message—whether vision or history or poetry—is in language appropriate to the time and place where they're given. God meets people where they are.

When Jesus came to earth, He didn't come as a twenty-first-century European or a twenty-first-century African. He came as a first-century Jew. He lived in Palestine, and He looked like the people there and dressed like the people there. He spoke their language and even used some of their jokes. That last point may sound strange, but when Joachim Jeremias, a biblical scholar, translated the

Greek of Matthew's Gospel back into Aramaic—the language that Jesus spoke—he discovered jokes, puns, and wordplays that Jesus used.

Why would Jesus say those kinds of things? Probably to meet people where they were. But there's another possibility too. Jesus seems to have used those kinds of things to make His sayings memorable. He wanted people to remember them. They'd be telling each other, "Oh, when Jesus was talking yesterday, He told this really funny story." Then they would share that story. They remembered the story and the teaching because of the way Jesus shared it. The same principles are illustrated in the way Jesus approached the seven churches of Revelation.

So, from the letters to the seven churches, we discover that Jesus knows all there is to know about us. He comes to each church with a full knowledge of what its members are like. He presents Himself in a way that they can appreciate, a way that they can understand. And if Jesus knows all about us before we even come to Him, there's no reason to hide from Him. There's no reason to be afraid to tell Him the truth. He comes in just the way that we need Him to come.

Jesus is amazing. He could choose to come to us in any number of ways but, according to the seven churches of Revelation, Jesus is careful to come to each church, each group of people, in just the way they need Him. He respects our uniqueness. He respects our differences. He made us unique. He made us different. And when He comes to us, He comes in a way that we each as individuals can appreciate.

None of us has the full picture of Jesus. You may have a PhD, but there's an awful lot that you don't know. Getting a PhD is kind of like digging a posthole in a farm field. You may know everything there is to know about what was in that hole, but there's a whole vast field around you that you haven't explored to that depth. So the more you learn in this life, the more you realize you don't know.

Here in Revelation's letters to the seven churches we learn that each of us knows something about Jesus if we've had a relationship with Him. But we don't know everything about Him. There's much that we don't know. And the fact that none of us has the full picture means we need each other. You need what I'm sharing in this book, and I need what you have learned. When we're open to learning from one another, we can learn more about God and come closer to Him. So the book of Revelation teaches us to be humble.

Best of all, however, the seven churches of Revelation teach us that Jesus loves us just the way we are. He meets us right where we are. And as we come to Jesus, He will give us what we need. He will lead us to where we need to go.

We could learn much more from the seven churches. For example, many people have applied them as a prophecy of stages in Christian history. But in this book we're focusing on the basics of understanding Revelation—the basic things we need to know in order to draw from Revelation the spiritual lessons God wants us to learn. We're looking at the core values of the book that are often overlooked.

And now we come to the most encouraging part of the messages to the seven churches. Jesus makes promises to each of the seven churches. But here's something I find fascinating: The first church gets one promise—the tree of life. The second church gets two—the crown of life and deliverance from the second death. The third church gets three—hidden manna, a white stone, and a new name. The fourth church gets four, the fifth church gets five, the sixth church gets six, and the seventh church, Laodicea, gets the promise that sums up all the promises, the promise to end all promises—that the overcomers in Laodicea will sit with Jesus on His throne. Those who sit with Jesus on His throne get everything, right? They inherit it all.

Promises to the Seven Churchs

Ephesus	• The right to eat from the tree of life
Smyrna	• The crown of life • Protection from the second death
Pergamum	• The hidden manna • A white stone • A new name
Thyatira	• Authority over the nations • Ability to rule with an iron scepter • Ability to dash their enemies to pieces • The morning star
Sardis	• The privilege of walking with Jesus • Garbed by God in white • Their names written in the book of life • Their names acknowledged before the Father • Their names acknowledged before angels
Philadelphia	• Protection from the hour of trial • Made pillars in the temple • Permanent residence in the temple • The name of God written on them • The name of the city of God written on them • Jesus' new name written on them
Laodicea	• The right to sit with Jesus on His throne

Here's what I take from all this: While the churches receive increasingly better promises, the messages to the churches become increasingly severe. The problems in the churches seem to be getting worse and worse. But the message is that the worse things get, the greater the grace and power that God exerts. As sin becomes increasingly powerful, the grace of God becomes increasingly powerful. So, the deeper the problems you have in life, the more powerfully is the grace of Jesus Christ applied, which means it can change your life.

The messages to the seven churches speak as powerfully to us today as they did in ancient times and throughout the course of history. The book of Revelation has a message that can change our hearts and our lives today.

A plan for the whole book

One of the challenges to understanding Revelation is that few people know how to approach it, how it's organized. But John leaves clues about how the book is organized and about what the key ideas in the visions are. One of those clues is found in verse 19 of chapter 1. This is one of the most important texts in the book because it lays out the plan of the whole book.

In verse 19, John is instructed to "Write . . . what you

have seen." Now, verse 11 says, "Write what you see." That's in the present tense: write what you see—what you *are seeing.* That means that John is to write what he's seeing while he's seeing it. But verse 19 says, "Write . . . what you *have seen.*" In other words, at this point the vision is complete. He has already seen it. So verse 19 is telling John to write out the entire vision.

And, according to this text, the entire vision is made up of two parts. Notice what the text says: "Write, therefore, what you have seen, namely, the things which are." In other words, Revelation includes things that spoke specifically to the churches that existed in Asia Minor when John wrote the book. But he was instructed to write also "the things which must happen after these things." The second major part of the book, then, concerns events that are future from the perspective of John's time.

So the book of Revelation has two parts. One part focuses particularly on the time in which John lived, and one part focuses on future events—events that will occur *after* John's time. It covers both "the things which are and the things which must happen after these things."

What are these things that are and the things that will happen after these things? John doesn't leave us in doubt. Look at chapter 4, verse 1. There Jesus says to John, "Come up here, and I will show you what must take place after these things." Compare that with the second part of chapter 1, verse 19: "Things which are about to happen after these things."

It seems that chapter 4, verse 1, is saying to John, "Now we have come to the part of the book that concerns the future, things that will happen after these things." Verse 1 begins that focus, and the rest of the book of Revelation focuses primarily on the things that would be future to John's day. Though there are flashbacks to the Cross, to the enthronement of Jesus, and even to events that occurred before Creation, the primary focus after chapter 4 is on future events.

That leaves one more question. What are "the things which are"? That would be what Revelation contains between chapter 1, verse 19, and chapter 4, verse 1—the letters to the seven churches. In that portion of Revelation, John focuses particularly on the situation of those seven churches and on the messages—the letters—that Jesus sends them. Yes, these are prophetic letters. They do have powerful implications for events down the line of history. But the immediate focus of the seven churches is on "the things which are."

So we see that careful attention to key texts of Revelation will help us discover how the book was structured in John's mind and in the mind of the One who gave him the vision. We also see that most of Revelation focuses particularly on the things that were to happen after John's day.

Duodirectionality: A literary strategy

I'm going to throw an unusual word at you here, one that I made up. The word is *duodirectionality*. Sounds kind of fancy, doesn't it? By duodirectionality, I mean simply "looking both ways."

I discovered this principle when I was searching through the Greek of the book of Revelation. I found that at crucial points in Revelation, the climax of one section points forward to the next. That is, instead of concluding one section and then introducing the next, John embeds the introduction of the next section into the conclusion of the previous one. These embedded conclusions "look both ways"—they summarize the preceding section while also sharing the key to what follows.

For example, in Revelation, the seven seals follow the seven churches. But John embedded the secret essential to understanding the seven seals in the climax that concludes the section on the seven churches. If you miss this cue, if you miss this duodirectional text, you probably won't understand the message God intends the seven seals to communicate.

Look at the text: "To the one who overcomes I will give to sit with Me on My throne, just as I overcame and sat down with My Father on His throne" (3:21). This text is the climax of the promises to those who overcome. In the end, they will sit with Jesus on His throne just as He overcame and sat down with the Father on His throne.

When did Jesus overcome?

He overcame at the Cross. He overcame at His resurrection. And then He ascended to heaven and joined the Father on His throne. So, those who overcome in Christ will one day join Him on His throne. That is the promise to the overcomers in Laodicea.

But here is where duodirectionality comes in. This climax verse also points forward. It points to chapters 4, 5, 6, and 7. The key to the seven seals is embedded within it.

Let's take a look. The climax verse says, "To the one who overcomes I will give to sit with Me on My throne, just as I overcame and sat down with My Father on His throne." Now think about chapters 4–7. Where in this section of Revelation do we find the Father's throne? It's in chapter 4. Where does Jesus join the Father on His throne? In chapter 5. Do the believers ever join Jesus on His throne? Yes, in chapter 7.

We see, then, that John has placed in chapter 3, verse 21, a nutshell summary of the basic points of chapters 4–7.

Revelation 4	Revelation 5	Revelation 6	Revelation 7
The Father's throne	Jesus joins the Father on His throne	The saints overcome	The saints join Jesus on His throne

He's unpacking for us the point of the seven seals. So the principle of duodirectionality provides a simple clue to understanding one of the most challenging parts of the book of Revelation.

But there's more to chapter 3, verse 21, something we haven't covered yet—the first part. The verse says, "*To the one who overcomes* I will give to sit with Me on My throne." To the one—present tense—who overcomes.

Who's that?

The readers of the book. It's you. It's me. Whenever anyone has read this book, they've been called to overcome as Christ overcame. They've been called to be faithful to God despite the trials that trouble them. They've been called to overcome. *We* are called to overcome.

And what is chapter 6 all about? It's about the saints overcoming from the time of Jesus to the end of time. Throughout the entire Christian era, from the time when Revelation was written to the end, the saints are in the process of overcoming.

Chapter 6 is one of the most challenging parts of Revelation. People have struggled to understand its meaning. But in chapter 3, verse 21, John has given us the key to understanding chapter 6. He tells us that the overcoming of the people of God is the key to what is going on in chapter 6. We'll come back to chapter 6 a little bit later, but for now, I just wanted you to see how the duodirectionality principle helps us understand more clearly what John says in this book.

Chapter Four

The Seven Seals

L ET'S MOVE now to the seven seals. We'll begin in Revelation 4. This chapter portrays a general worship scene in heaven, and all this worship is centered on the throne of God. The word *throne* appears nineteen times in chapters 4 and 5.

Why do I call chapter 4 a general worship scene? There are several clues in the text. Verse 2 says, "Immediately I became in the Spirit, and behold a throne was there in heaven, and there was One sitting on the throne." This verse says, "A throne was there." When Daniel described a throne scene in heaven, he wrote, "Thrones were set up" (Daniel 7:9). Daniel portrayed the beginning of a throne scene in heaven, a scene of judgment. But Revelation 4 doesn't portray the beginning of the throne scene that it describes. John doesn't say the throne was set up. In his scene, it was simply there.

In other words, chapter 4 portrays ongoing activity. It's a description of what has been going on in heaven and what continues to go on there. Notice verse 8: "And they [the four living creatures] have no rest day or night, saying, 'Holy, holy, holy.' " That sounds like ongoing action to me. Verses 9 and 10: "And whenever the living creatures express glory and honor and thankfulness . . . the twenty-four elders fall down before the One sitting on the throne and worship."

So in chapter 4, the throne "was there." And there's a constant refrain—"Holy, holy, holy." Chapter 4 doesn't portray some specific event or change of activity. It is simply a description of what is going on constantly in heaven.

What's the key to this whole thing? What's at the center? Everything in this chapter is centered on the throne of God. Things happen in front of the throne, around the throne, above the throne, and in the midst of the throne.

A moment of crisis

In chapter 5, however, we move from a general scene to a very specific scene, a specific point in time. The general description stops, and we see a crisis arise. Look at what the text says: "And I saw to the right of the One sitting on the throne a scroll, written within and on the back, sealed with seven seals. And I saw a powerful angel proclaiming with a loud voice, 'Who is worthy to open the scroll, namely, to break its seals?' And no one in heaven or on earth or under the earth was able to open the scroll or to look into it" (verses 1–3)

So, God is sitting on the throne. He has a scroll in His hand or at His side (depending on how one understands the Greek). An angel cries out, "Who is worthy to open the scroll?" And no one can do it. No one in heaven or on earth or under the earth can open the scroll. This is amazing! Remember that the scroll is related to God, and He has it, yet He can't open it! This is a symbolic way of representing a huge problem—a problem so big that, in a sense, even God can't solve it. At least He can't solve it in the normal run of things. The problem can't be solved until that scroll is opened.

Verses 4 and 5 show John's reaction to the situation and then heaven's response to his anguish. "And I wept much because no one was found worthy to open the scroll or to look into it. And one of the elders said to me, 'Do not weep, the Lion of the tribe of Judah, the Root of David, has overcome to open the scroll and its seven seals.' " Jesus Christ is the real Lion King. He is the One who can open the scroll. He is the One who will solve the problem in the universe.

But you say, "Wait a minute. How can there be a

problem that God can't solve, yet Jesus can?"

Actually, God *can* solve the problem. He chooses to solve it through Jesus Christ, through the Lamb. Look at verse 6: "And I saw, in the middle of the throne and of the four living creatures, and in the middle of the elders, a Lamb standing as if it had been slaughtered, having seven horns and seven eyes, which are the seven spirits of God that have already been sent into all the earth."

Who can open the scroll? Who can solve the universal problem? The Lamb can. What kind of lamb? A slaughtered lamb. It is the cross of Jesus Christ that is in view here. The problem in the universe is solved by the cross of Jesus Christ.

The Lamb is with God on the throne. Chapter 5 pictures the Lamb being worshiped along with God. The Lamb receives praise with God. The Lamb is divine. The Lamb *is* God.

However, the Lamb is also slaughtered. The Lamb can die. The very concept of "Lamb" shows the humanness of Jesus Christ. Lambs are vulnerable, and so is He. He is slain. It is the combination of Jesus' divinity and His vulnerable humanity that is the key.

This tells us why the God who is sitting on the throne can't open the scroll—because only Someone who is both God and man, who is both human and divine, can open the scroll. There is only one Person in the entire universe who can resolve this universal problem, and that is Jesus Christ. The Lamb, the Lion-Lamb of Revelation, the real Lion King, Jesus Christ. He is worthy because He is both human and divine and because He was slain.

Here, the book of Revelation highlights the centrality of the cross of Jesus Christ. As I said earlier, Revelation uses Old Testament language, and as a result, it sometimes sounds different than the rest of the New Testament. But the heart of Revelation's message is Jesus Christ. At its heart, this book has the same kinds of themes and theology as the rest of the New Testament. The purpose of chapter 5 is to highlight the cross of Jesus Christ and its centrality in resolving the biggest problem in the universe.

The key issue

So now we know who will solve the problem. But we still haven't explored exactly what that problem is beyond getting the scroll open. What made the angel so concerned about finding someone who could open the scroll? What was in that scroll anyway? What is the key issue of this chapter and, therefore, of the universe?

The key word in chapters 4 and 5 identifies what the

key issue is. The key word is *throne.* John used the Greek word for "throne" fourteen times in chapter 4 and five times in chapter 5.

Americans aren't used to thrones. The closest one can come to a throne in the United States is the president's chair in the Oval Office, the one behind the president's desk. People from all over the world—prime ministers, kings, and queens—come into the Oval Office, and there the president sits in his seat. Even with those connections, that chair doesn't mean much to us. To the ancients, however, the throne was a symbol of power, a symbol of authority. The one who sits on the throne has the right to rule.

Interestingly, many ancient thrones were actually couches. There was room for two or three people to sit on them. In the ancient context, it was possible for the king to elevate people to high authority next to himself. So when John wrote that Jesus sat with His Father on His throne (3:21), he was saying that the Father was giving Jesus authority to rule over the universe. That also tells us that one day we will have an amazing privilege. As "overcomers," we will sit with Jesus on His throne. The book of Revelation says the people of God will be kings and priests (1:6; 5:10). There's a sense in which the promise God has for the overcomer includes sharing to some extent in ruling the universe.

So, the throne is the key. The Old Testament background of Revelation 4 and 5 is all about thrones. Daniel 7 gives us Daniel's vision of the throne of God. Ezekiel 1 also contains a vision of the throne of God. Isaiah 6 pictures the prophet standing before God's throne and hearing the song, "Holy, holy, holy." In 1 Kings 22, Micaiah has a vision of the throne of God and the heavenly courts. And Exodus 19 portrays God as enthroned on Mount Sinai. The common denominator of all five passages is the throne of God, and Revelation 4 and 5 allude to all five of these Old Testament passages. In fact, 30 percent of the words in chapter 4 are drawn from Ezekiel 1. It's amazing how similar the two passages are.

What's the key issue in Revelation 4 and 5? It is the matter of who is in charge of the universe. Is God in charge, or is someone else in charge?

We may be tempted to think that's a stupid question. Evidently, it's not. Revelation is drawing the curtain back just a little bit and telling us that people are questioning God's rule of the universe. Has He always been just? Is He truly worthy to rule? How can He be considered just and loving when there's so much suffering in this world?

The spiritual beauty of this passage is that it's telling us these are legitimate questions. We have the right to ask them.

So, the throne of God is, in some sense, in jeopardy. If God wanted to, He could rip open the scroll and say, "I'm in charge here. I'll do whatever I please. And I'll eliminate anyone who disagrees with Me." But that's not what God does. He chooses not to resolve the issue by force. Instead, through the cross of Jesus Christ, He patiently and sacrificially demonstrates His right to rule. The One who rules the universe dies for the sake of His creatures.

Would you trust a ruler who would be willing to die for your benefit? Who would you find it easier to trust: a president who, in sending his country to war, also sent his own son or daughter into the fray, or one who didn't? The God who rules the universe was willing to sacrifice His Son, willing to die. We may not understand everything that is going on in the universe. We may not understand what God is doing. We may not understand why so much suffering goes on here. But the book of Revelation tells us that God solved the issue at the cross of Jesus Christ. At the Cross we begin to understand the government of God. At the Cross God demonstrated His right to rule.

There are basically two ways to rule in this world: by right or by might. Many dictators, such as Adolf Hitler and Saddam Hussein, ruled by might. They said, "I have all the power. I can make everyone follow me. I'm strong enough to force them to do what I want them to do."

That's one kind of rulership. If God ruled that way, we'd all have reason to fear. But the book of Revelation teaches us that God rules like a lamb. A slain Lamb, willing to die for His subjects. There are troubling events everywhere on this earth. And even more troubling events are yet to come. But Revelation tells us, "Don't worry. In the end God will set it right. He will be just and will be seen to be just."

Chapter 15, verse 3, pictures the people who have come to trust God as saying, "Just and true are your ways, O God." In the end, God is proclaimed as the One who is fair and the One who did what is right. God rules because He is right. He allows only those things that would be in the long-term best interest of the universe, for the good of all concerned.

So chapters 4 and 5 are concerned about power. But they aren't just about this earth. They aren't just about you and me. They're about the great controversy between Christ and Satan. The cross of Jesus Christ is about reconciling the universe with God. We get hints of that in chapter 5, and that message becomes more powerful in chapter 12 and beyond. So the scene portrayed in chapters 4 and 5 is an introduction not only to the seven seals, but, in a sense, to the rest of the book of Revelation. All the rest of the book is grounded in these issues of the throne and of the Cross, of Jesus Christ, and the gospel.

The four horsemen

Chapter 6 begins with the famous four horsemen of Revelation.

And I saw when the Lamb opened the first of the seven seals, and I heard one of the four living creatures saying with a voice like thunder, "Come!" And I saw, and behold, a white horse, and the one sitting on it had a bow. A victory crown was given to him and he went out conquering and in order that he might conquer. And when He opened the second seal, I heard the second living creature saying, "Come!" And another horse, a fiery red one, went out, and the one sitting on it was given to take peace from the earth, in order that they might slaughter one another, and a great sword was given to him. And when He opened the third seal, I heard the third living creature saying, "Come!" And I saw, and behold, a black horse, and the one sitting on it had a scale for weighing in his hand. And I heard, as it were, a voice in the middle of the four living creatures saying, "A quart of wheat for a denarius and three quarts of barley for a denarius; and do not harm the oil and the wine." And when He opened the fourth seal, I heard the voice of the fourth living creature saying, "Come!" And I saw, and behold, a pale horse, and the one sitting on it was named Death, and Hades followed after him. And they were given authority over a fourth of the earth, to kill with the sword, with famine, with pestilence, and by the beasts of the earth (6:1–8).

Chapter 6 pictures four horses. Verses 1 and 2 tell us about a white horse. Then a red horse appears (verses 3, 4). The word translated "red" here actually means "fire." So this horse is a fiery-colored horse, like a reddish flame. Next there's a black horse (verses 5, 6). And finally a pale horse (verses 7, 8). The word "pale" is translated from the Greek word from which was derived our word *chlorine.* In other words, this horse is a sickly yellow-green— the color some people become when they are extremely sick and about to die. So there's a white horse, a red horse, a black horse, and a pale horse.

When these horses and their riders go out into the world, destruction follows. What is this all about?

To understand what Revelation is saying here, we

need to go to the Old Testament. Let's start with Leviticus 26:21, 22, 25, 26.

> If you remain hostile toward me and refuse to listen to me, I will multiply your afflictions seven times over, as your sins deserve. I will send wild animals against you, and they will rob you of your children, destroy your cattle and make you so few in number that your roads will be deserted. . . .
>
> And I will bring the sword upon you to avenge the breaking of the covenant. When you withdraw into your cities, I will send a plague among you, and you will be given into enemy hands. When I cut off your supply of bread, ten women will be able to bake your bread in one oven, and they will dole out the bread by weight. You will eat, but you will not be satisfied (NIV).

Leviticus 26 contains what are known as the "curses of the covenant." In other words, if Israel as a nation didn't obey God, these are the consequences they would experience. There would be suffering, there would be difficulty, and finally they would be invaded and exiled.

The language of Leviticus is also the language of Revelation 6. But there's also language from Zechariah

1 and 6 as well. In Zechariah 1:8–10, the prophet says, "During the night I had a vision—and there before me was a man riding a red horse! . . . Behind him were red, brown and white horses. . . . Then the man standing among the myrtle trees explained, 'They are the ones the LORD has sent to go throughout the earth' " (NIV).

In Zechariah, the four horses are sent by God. Are the four horses in Revelation 6 also sent by God or do they represent human efforts or attacks? That's an important interpretive distinction. In Zechariah, they are clearly sent by God: "This is what the LORD Almighty says: 'I am very jealous for Jerusalem and Zion, but I am very angry with the nations that feel secure. I was only a little angry, but they added to the calamity' " (Zechariah 1:14, 15, NIV).

In the context of Zechariah 1, the four horses represent judgment. They go out to judge those who have oppressed the people of God. This is the issue here. God doesn't punish people out of irritation or because He feels like it. No. God is very focused here. He says, "My people are hurting." And He sends these horses out to judge those who have been hurting His people.

In Zechariah 6 we see more of the same: "I looked up again—and there before me were four chariots coming out from between two mountains—mountains of bronze! The first chariot had red horses, the second black, the third white, and the fourth dappled—all of them powerful. . . . The angel answered me, 'These are the four spirits of heaven, going out from standing in the presence of the Lord of the whole world.' . . . Then he called to me, 'Look, those going toward the north country have given my Spirit rest in the land of the north' " (verses 1–8, NIV).

The land of the north is Babylon. That was the nation that persecuted the people of God in the decades before Zechariah was written. These horses were sent as covenant judgments of God. When the people of God disobey Him, they suffer sword, famine, pestilence, and so on. But when the people of God themselves are being oppressed, God judges their opponents—again with the sword, famine, pestilence, and so forth, represented in Zechariah by these horses of judgment.

All of this is background to Revelation 6. And here's the key. In the Old Testament, these covenant passages are national. It's as if God were saying, "If you as a nation obey Me, you will prosper. If you as a nation disobey Me, you will suffer judgments; you will suffer consequences." But in chapter 6, there is a difference. In chapter 6, the white horse seems to represent the gospel. (The symbols connected with that horse are all positive, unlike those related to the other three horses.) As the gospel goes out to the world, it goes out conquering people's hearts, leading them to God, bringing them under His rulership.

Chapter 5 establishes that God is the rightful Ruler of the universe. He is also the rightful Ruler of this world in Christ. The Lamb is the just One, the One who is worthy. But many people reject His rule. And so, as the gospel (the white horse) goes forth, it invites people to become citizens of the heavenly kingdom. However, the white horse is followed by the red, black, and pale horses of God's judgments. As people receive the gospel, they also receive the blessings that God offers from the Cross. On the other hand, those who reject the gospel suffer progressively greater consequences as they harden in their rejection. This is what the four horsemen of Revelation are all about. They are grounded in the Old Testament covenant curses, but in Revelation, these curses are the consequences of rejecting the gospel.

The 144,000

As we work our way through the seven seals of chapter 6, we come closer and closer to the end of time. The four horses began in the early part of the Christian era. Chapter 6 climaxes with the questioning challenge at the end of the chapter. It says, "And they said to the mountains and the rocks, 'Fall on us and hide us from the face of the

One sitting on the throne, and from the wrath of the Lamb. For the great day of His wrath has come, and who is able to stand?' " (verses 16, 17).

According to Revelation 3:21, the messages in chapter 6 are all about the people of God and their struggle to overcome in the course of Christian history. In this chapter, we work our way through Christian history, and when we come to the very end of time, portrayed at the end of the chapter, the challenging question is raised, "Who will be able to stand?"

That question still dangles at the end of chapter 6. It provides the context for chapter 7, in which we find the fascinating portrayal of the 144,000 and the great multitude. In other words, chapter 7 answers the question "Who will be able to stand?" Interpreters have gone a little crazy with this chapter. People want to know who the 144,000 are. The bottom line regarding the 144,000 is that they are the people who will be able to stand in the final day of God.

However, this isn't the end of the matter. The great multitude of the latter half of chapter 7 are also the answer to the question. They're also the people who are able to stand in the final day.

Does that mean God's people will be divided at the end of time—like Catholics and Protestants? Is that what the text is saying?

No. Actually, these two groups are symbols of the one people of God. Let me explain.

Another of the literary strategies that we find in the book of Revelation casts light on chapter 7. At times, what John hears and what he sees are different and yet are the same. Chapter 1, verse 10 reads, "I was in the Spirit during the Lord's Day, and I heard a loud voice like a trumpet behind me." What does he hear? A trumpet. But when he looks, what does he see? Note the following verses: He sees Jesus speaking to him. The trumpet and the voice of Jesus are very different images, yet they represent the same thing.

In chapter 5, verse 5, one of the elders calls his attention to Lion of the tribe of Judah. When John looks, does he see the Lion? No. He says, "Then I saw a Lamb, looking as if it had been slain." John never sees the Lion of Judah. He hears the elder say "lion," but when he looks, he sees the Lamb. Do the lion and the lamb represent two different things in this passage? No. They are two different symbols for Jesus.

In chapter 17, John is told, "I will show you the judgment of the great prostitute who sits on many waters" (verse 1). But when he looks, he says, "I saw a woman sitting on a scarlet beast" (verse 3). He hears that she is sitting on many waters, but he sees her sitting on the beast.

As we'll see later, these two things are different symbols that represent the same entity.

Finally, notice chapter 21, verse 9: "One of the seven angels who had the seven bowls . . . said, 'Come I will show you the bride, the wife of the Lamb.' " Are you expecting that John will see a beautiful woman? Sorry. "He carried me away in the Spirit to a great and high mountain and showed me the Holy City, Jerusalem" (verse 10). The bride and the city are very different symbols, but they represent the same thing: the people of God at the end of time.

Back to our passage, chapter 7. John never sees the 144,000; he only hears the number (verse 4). When he looks, he sees a great multitude that no one can number (verse 9). The hearing/seeing clue indicates that these two groups symbolize the one people of God at the end of time, just like the Bride of chapter 21 and the Lion/Lamb of chapter 5.

So, during the final crisis of earth's history the question is asked, "Who will be able to stand?" The answer comes in chapter 7: the end-time people of God will be able to stand. And the 144,000 and the great multitude are two ways of describing these faithful people of God—those who have overcome by the gospel, those who have overcome by the blood of the Lamb.

Seven Keys • Part Three

Chapter Five

The Seven Trumpets

C HAPTERS 8 to 11 of the book of Revelation focus on the seven trumpets. This is probably the most difficult portion of Revelation to understand. If you asked twelve students of Revelation what the seven trumpets are all about, you'd probably get at least thirteen different opinions. I don't intend to explain every detail of the trumpets. But the keys of interpretation that we covered in the first chapter will help us unlock some meanings that you might not have seen before.

I noted earlier John's use of what I called duodirectionality—his practice of inserting into the climax of one sequence a key to what follows. That's true of the seven trumpets: the key to understanding the trumpets is found in the middle of the seven seals. "And when he opened the fifth seal, I saw under the altar the souls of those who had been slaughtered on account of the Word of God and on account of the testimony which they had maintained.

And they cried out with a loud voice saying, 'How long, O Lord, the Holy and True One, do You not judge and avenge our blood on those who live on the earth?' " (6:9, 10).

This text expresses the consequence of centuries of persecution, centuries of suffering—of all that is summed up in the four horsemen. The martyred saints, symbolized as being under the altar, are crying out for judgment on those who live on the earth. The activities of the four horsemen have hurt the saints deeply. This confirms what we noticed before: the seven seals, particularly those in chapter 6, are about the experience of the saints, of those who have been exposed to the story of Jesus. The white horse represents the triumph of the gospel: people receive it and enter into the kingdom of the Lamb. The other three horses represent progressive rejection of the gospel, and the consequences of that rejection. Those who reject the gospel begin to fight each other, and they also harm the people of God. The climax of those four horsemen is the scene of chapter 6, verses 9–11. The saints, under the altar, cry out for God to do something about their unjust suffering.

Have you ever cried out to God, asking Him to do something? Did it seem that your life was out of control? God always does what is right, but the people of God don't always understand what He is doing.

"Those who live on the earth"

The climax passage in the fifth seal includes the introduction to the seven trumpets. Note the text that appears right in the middle of the trumpets: "And I saw and I heard a vulture flying in midheaven saying with a loud voice, 'Woe, woe, woe, to those who live on the earth because of the rest of the sounds of the three angels who are about to blow their trumpets' " (8:13).

Do you remember that phrase, "those who live on the earth"? In the fifth seal, the souls under the altar cried out, "How long, O Lord, . . . do You not judge and avenge . . . *those who live on the earth?*" (6:10). Revelation consistently uses this expression, "those who live on the earth," of the opponents of God, those who have persecuted the true followers of God. When the saints cry out to God for justice, His answer to their prayer comes in the trumpets. Chapter 8, verse 13 says, "Woe to those who live on the earth because of the rest of the sounds of the three angels who are about to blow their trumpets." The trumpets portray how God has been and will continue to work within history to pass judgment on those who have hurt His people.

This message becomes even clearer at the beginning of the trumpets in chapter 8, verses 3–6: verses 3 and 4 say, "Another angel came and stood upon the altar, having a golden censer. And much incense was given to him in order that he might add it to the prayers of all the saints upon the golden altar before the throne. And the smoke of the altar went up, along with the prayers of the saints, out of the hand of the angel before God."

The introduction to the trumpets doesn't seem like a call to judgment. It reads more like a worship scene. It's about the prayers of the saints. It's about incense rising from the golden altar in the sanctuary. But the cloud of incense acts like an umbrella, preventing the negative judgments of the trumpets from falling on God's own people. I believe this incense symbolizes the righteousness of Christ. The righteousness of Christ covers the people of God and keeps them safe.

So, the prayers of the saints rise up at the beginning of the seven trumpets as they did in chapter 6, where the saints—the souls under the altar—also cry out for justice. Then "the angel took the censer and filled it with the fire of the altar and threw it to the earth. . . . And the seven angels who have the seven trumpets prepared to blow them" (8:5, 6).

Here's the sequence then: The prayers of the saints— the cries from under the altar—come up to God combined with the incense of the altar. When God hears those prayers, the trumpets begin to blow. In other words, the seven trumpets are God's response to the prayers of the saints for judgment on those who are hurting His people.

Often in the course of history God's people have cried out, "How long, O Lord? How long is this injustice going to go on? How long do we have to suffer like this?" The answer of the book of Revelation is, "If you only knew. Right in the middle of history, even while your eyes are blind to it, I am already acting to deliver you. I am acting to bring consequences to those who have been unjust."

The trumpets tell the abused that the abusers have already begun to come under God's judgment. We ourselves may not see God's hand at work in this life. Everything may seem to be unfair now. But the day of judgment is coming when the curtain will be rolled away and everything set right. The beautiful thing about the book of Revelation is that in the midst of this incredible apocalyptic symbolism we catch a glimpse of what will happen in that end-time judgment. Revelation opens a window into God's purpose to set everything right. We may not see it now, but we can learn to trust in God now. The book of Revelation helps us do just that. It provides a solid place to stand in the midst of life's most difficult problems.

The pain of rejection

Not long ago, a woman came up to me and said, "Do you remember me?"

She looked vaguely familiar to me, but I couldn't place her.

This woman said a few years ago I preached a sermon on rejection. After the service, she had come up to me and said my sermon had really meant a lot to her because her husband had divorced her recently. Then she asked, "Do you remember what you told me on that occasion?"

I couldn't remember, so she said, "You told me, 'Now you can understand what Jesus went through on the cross—in fact, you may be able to understand it better than anyone else here.'

"That idea just seized me," she said. "I suddenly realized that I'd been thinking only about myself. But God had allowed me to have an experience that could draw me closer to Jesus if I would let it. I could understand more deeply what He suffered for me."

She told me she had never been an outgoing person; she was rather timid by nature. Yet in spite of the great rejection she had suffered, God had made her bold in the blood of Jesus Christ. "The thought of what Jesus suffered on the cross turned my life around," she said. "Ever since that day, I've not been focused on myself. Instead, I've been reaching out to others. I've even preached in places like Russia, and I've led people to Christ."

As we study Revelation, we discover that in many subtle ways the heart of the book is about Jesus Christ and the Cross. This book isn't the revelation of Middle Eastern oil. It isn't the revelation of worldly politics. It's the revelation of Jesus Christ. And when we rightly understand this book, we will have a clearer picture of Jesus— even in the seven trumpets of Revelation.

The basic theme of the seven trumpets is that God is passing judgment on those who have turned from the worship of God, those who have hurt His people. This is stated plainly right in the middle of the trumpets: "And it was told to them that they should not hurt the grass of the earth or any green thing or any tree, only those men who did not have the seal of God on their foreheads" (9:4). "And the rest of the human race, those who were not killed by these plagues, did not repent of the works of their hands in order that they might not worship demons or idols of gold, silver, brass, stone, and wood" (9:20).

The seven seals are about God's people; the seven trumpets, on the other hand, are all about the wicked. The seals deal with people's reaction to the gospel—their acceptance or rejection of it. The trumpets focus specifically on those who have rejected the gospel and who have harmed the people who preach the gospel. As difficult as the details of the trumpets may be to understand, their fundamental message has to do with judgments on the wicked.

Historical apocalyptic

The messages to the seven churches appear to be in letter form, yet they are also prophecies. There are aspects of these messages that are prophetic about the experience of the church down through history. But prophetic letters are a more open-ended type of expression than apocalyptic tends to be.

The seals are a bit more difficult to categorize, but the best research indicates that the seals are a form of classical prophecy, the kind of prophecies you find in Isaiah and Jeremiah, and even in Matthew 24, where Jesus talks about the future. Classical prophecies point to the future, but they don't project a single line of interpretation as most apocalyptic prophecy does. You can apply classical prophecies to different times and places, depending on the circumstances. There have been many times when the people of God have cried out for justice. So while the seven seals are prophetic with regard to Christian history, they can be applied to more than one situation.

The trumpets are different, however. I believe they represent the genre known as historical apocalyptic. They are like Daniel 2 and 7, where the prophet projects a sequence of events from his day down through history right to the end. The text contains a clear indication of this. For instance, the trumpets allude to the Old Testament extensively. They seem to echo the days of Creation. They also echo the plagues of the Exodus and the battle of Jericho, and they seem to refer to the Feast of Trumpets and the jubilee concept.

The five major Old Testament sources used in Revelation 4 and 5 have one thing in common—thrones. These five Old Testament sources related to the trumpets also have one thing in common—sequences of events. The seven days of Creation occur one after the other. The ten plagues of the Exodus occur one after the other. The same is true of the seven days of marching around Jericho, the seven months of the Hebrew year that lead up to the Feast of Trumpets, and so forth.

So it seems that the author of Revelation wants us to see the seven trumpets as portraying a sequence of events. The questions we have to answer are when does the sequence of events portrayed by the trumpets begin and when does it end?

I think the starting point of the seven trumpets is made clear right at the beginning of Revelation's description of them: "Another angel came and stood upon the altar, having a golden censer. And much incense was given to him in order that he might add it to the prayers of all the saints upon the golden altar before the throne. And the smoke of the altar went up, along with the prayers of the saints, out of the hand of the angel before God" (8:3, 4).

The fundamental image accompanying the blowing of the trumpets is the prayers of the saints. While the trumpets are sounding, the saints are praying for justice. They are communicating with God, and God is responding to their prayers. The beginning point of the trumpets, then, would seem to be the beginning of that intercession. And historically, intercession follows from the cross of Jesus Christ. So the cross of Jesus Christ, His resurrection, His ascension to heaven—these events are foundational to the seven trumpets. The trumpets begin to sound after the crucifixion of Christ and His ascension to heaven— in other words, they begin at the same time as do the seven seals.

What's the endpoint? That seems clear from chapter 11, verses 15–17: "The seventh angel blew his trumpet, and there were loud voices in heaven which were speaking, 'The kingdom of this world has become the kingdom of our Lord and of His Christ, and He will reign forever and ever.' And the twenty-four elders, who are sitting on their thrones before God, fell upon their faces and worshiped God, saying, 'We give thanks to You, Lord God Almighty, who is and who was, because You have taken hold of Your great power and begun to reign.' "

Now, if you've studied the book of Revelation, you know that God is the One whom this book usually characterizes as "the One who is, and who was, and *who is to come.*" Why is the phrase *"is to come"* missing here? Because at this point God's kingdom has already come. In other words, the seventh trumpet brings us to the end of human history. This means that the seven trumpets of Revelation represent a sequence of events running through history. They begin at the beginning of the Christian era and run to the end of time, the return of Christ.

The close of probation

Revelation also seems to indicate that the seven trumpets encompass the close of human probation. That's the point when there'll be no more presentation of the gospel, no more conversions. Look carefully at Revelation 10:7. "But in the days of the sounding of the seventh angel, when he is about to sound, the mystery of God is finished, which He proclaimed as good news through His servants the prophets." The seventh angel brings the trumpet to his mouth and he takes in a breath. The text says that he is "about to sound." At that instant, however, just before the sounding of the seventh trumpet, the mystery of God is finished.

What is the "mystery of God"? This phrase is frequently used in the New Testament to describe the gospel—see, for example, Romans 16:25–27 and Ephesians 3:4–6. In other words, the mystery of God is the proclamation of the gospel. Revelation 10:7 says the "mystery of God" that "is finished" is the mystery that He "proclaimed as good news" to His servants the prophets. I use the phrase "proclaimed as good news" to translate a single word, the verb form of the noun *gospel*. The mystery of God had been "gospelized"—proclaimed as good news. That proclamation of the gospel ends just before the seventh trumpet. So the close of probation occurs just as the seventh angel is about to sound.

In the trumpets, then, you have a sequence of events running from the Cross right up to the close of probation and the end of earth's history. Some people have noticed, however, that chapter 8, verse 5, at the beginning of the trumpets, sounds a lot like a close of probation, "And the angel took the censer and filled it with the fire of the altar and threw it to the earth. And there were thunders and noises and lightnings and an earthquake."

The censer symbolizes intercession. The throwing of it to the earth certainly does seem to be a close-of-probation image representing the end of intercession. However, in this opening passage of the trumpets, you have two types of images: the incense and the altar representing intercession, and the throwing down of the censer, which represents judgment. So, intercession and judgment go on simultaneously right up to the close of probation in chapter 10, verse 7.

How do chapters 10 and 11 fit into all of this? They seem to be a part of the sixth trumpet because they come in between the fifth and the seventh trumpets. Notice what chapter 10, verses 5–7 says, "The angel which I saw standing on the sea and on the land raised his right hand to heaven and swore by the One who lives forever and ever—who created heaven and the things which are in it, the earth and the things which are in it and the sea and the things which are in it—'Time will be no more.' But in the days of the sounding of the seventh angel, when he is about to sound, the mystery of God is finished, which He proclaimed as good news through His servants the prophets."

This text tells us that "time will be no more." If you

study this text carefully, you'll discover that this "time" is prophetic time. It's the time periods of Daniel—times like the 1,260 days, the 1,290 days, and the 1,335 days. Revelation 10 points to a time in history when those prophetic sequences have come to a close and we have entered the time of the end.

In Daniel, the time of the end is the very last period of earth's history. Revelation 10 and 11 take us to the time of the end. At that time John would prophesy again (see 10:11). In other words, his prophecy, the book of Revelation, would attract worldwide attention. In a sense, this book is part of the fulfillment of that prophecy. Chapter 11, verses 1–6, seem to move back in time to the middle of Daniel's time prophecies (Revelation 11:2, 3), but then, in chapter 11, verses 7–13, the focus returns to the time of the end.

Chapter 11 also portrays the final proclamation of the gospel. Verses 12 and 13 say, "And they [the two witnesses] heard a loud voice from heaven saying to them, 'Come up here.' And they ascended to heaven in a cloud and their enemies saw them. And in that hour there was a great earthquake and a tenth of the city fell. Seven thousand people were killed by the earthquake, and the remnant became afraid, and gave glory to the God of heaven."

Notice that point: "the remnant became afraid, and

gave glory to the God of heaven." This reminds us of chapter 14, verse 7. There, earth's final call is to "fear God and give glory to Him, because the hour of His judgment has come." So chapter 11, verses 12, 13, give the appropriate response to the final proclamation to the gospel: "Fear God and give glory to Him." In this way, chapter 11, verses 12, 13, set the stage for chapters 12 through 14, which portray the final events of earth's history.

Duodirectional ordering of Revelation 12–22

It's much harder to determine the structure of the second half of Revelation than it is the first half. In fact, most commentators disagree as to how the second half of the book is structured. But in verse 18 of chapter 11, John has revealed that structure to us.

Revelation 11:18, another duodirectional text, is not only the climax to the seven trumpets, but also a nutshell summary of everything that follows in the book. This verse says, "The nations were angry, and Your wrath has come, and the time to judge the dead and to reward Your servants the prophets, and the saints and those who fear Your name, both the small and the great, and to destroy those who are destroying the earth."

This verse has four major elements: "the nations were angry," "the time to judge the dead," "to reward Your servants," and "to destroy those who are destroying the earth." All these elements anticipate crucial parts of chapters 12 through 22. Chapter 12, verse 17, picks up

---

Duodirectional Ordering of Revelation 12–22

"[1] The nations were angry, and [2] Your wrath has come, and [3] the time to judge the dead and [4] to reward Your servants the prophets, and the saints and those who fear Your name, both the small and the great, and [3] to destroy those who are destroying the earth" (Revelation 11:18).

[1] Revelation 12–14: The Dragon's War (see 12:17)

[2] Revelation 15–18: The Wrath of God (see 15:1)

[3] Revelation 19; 20: Final Judgment on Wickedness (see 20:12)

[4] Revelation 21; 22: Final Reward of the Righteous (see 22:11)

"the nations were angry" element, saying "the dragon was angry." Chapter 15, verse 1, speaks of "the wrath of God," which corresponds to "Your wrath has come." Chapter 20, verse 12, talks about the judgment of the dead. And in Chapter 22, verse 12, God says, "My reward is with me."

From chapter 11, verse 18, we learn, then, that chapters 12–14 are all about the dragon's war, and chapters 15–18 are about God's response to the dragon's attack. Recognizing these themes helps us see the major turns of the final battle of earth's history: the dragon attacks, and

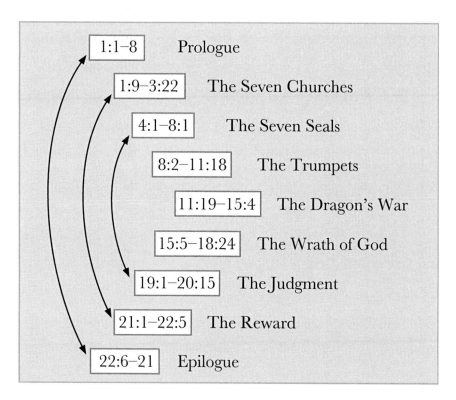

1:1–8	Prologue
1:9–3:22	The Seven Churches
4:1–8:1	The Seven Seals
8:2–11:18	The Trumpets
11:19–15:4	The Dragon's War
15:5–18:24	The Wrath of God
19:1–20:15	The Judgment
21:1–22:5	The Reward
22:6–21	Epilogue

God responds. Then, chapters 19 and 20 talk about the final judgment of the wicked, and, finally, in chapters 21 and 22, we see the reward of the saints, the New Jerusalem.

On the preceding page we see a summary of the structure of the book—the chiasm that we talked about earlier. In the next chapter, I want to zero in on the central part of the chiastic structure. Chapters 12 through 14 picture the dragon's war, in which the wicked forces in the world attack the people of God. But the main thrust of the section that follows (chapters 15–18) describes the "wrath of God" in response to those attacks. Following these, there are the final judgments on the wicked (chapters 19, 20), and, finally, the reward of the saints (chapters 21, 22).

We'll turn next to chapters 12 through 14, the dragon's war.

Chapter Six

The Dragon's War

WE MOVE now to the central part of the book of Revelation, chapters 12 through 14. We'll begin with chapter 12.

Like the trumpets, the content of chapter 12 starts at the time of Jesus and reaches all the way to the end. This chapter covers all of Christian history in three big stages.

> ## **Three Stages of Christian History**
>
> Stage 1: The time of Jesus and His disciples (Revelation 12:5, 10, 11)
>
> Stage 2: The church in the desert (Revelation 12:14–16)
>
> Stage 3: The dragon and the remnant (Revelation 12:17)

Stage 1 is the time of Jesus and His disciples. Remember: what John saw and wrote down is symbolic, and there's an underlying New Testament gospel message through it all. Chapter 12, verse 5, says, "And she gave birth to a Son, a male Child. . . . And her Child was snatched up to God and to His Throne." That Child, of course, is Jesus.

Chapter 12, verses 10, 11, are also part of stage 1. It says, " 'Now have come salvation, and strength, and the kingdom of our God, and the authority of His Christ, for the accuser of our brothers . . . has been cast down.' And they overcame him by the blood of the Lamb and the word of their testimony." In these texts we see a reference to Jesus, His birth, His ascension to heaven, and His enthronement in heaven, and an assurance that we can overcome the devil's assaults when we apply the blood of the Lamb.

Stage 2 covers the broad expanse of Christian history, a time when things didn't go well for committed believers. This stage pictures the church in the desert: "The woman was given the two wings of a great eagle in order that she might fly from the presence of the serpent into the desert . . . for a time, times, and half a time. And the serpent spewed water like a flooding river out of its mouth. . . . And the earth helped the woman. It opened its mouth and swallowed up the flood which the dragon spewed out of his mouth" (12:14–16).

The woman represents the church, God's true and faithful people, and the dragon represents Satan and all his followers on earth. This passage is another hint regarding how much the faithful people of God suffered in the course of so-called Christian history. So stage 2, looking forward with a prophetic eye, lets John know that the church will bear the brunt of Satan's anger.

Then comes stage 3, the final stage of this chapter. Chapter 12, verse 17, says, "And the dragon was angry with the woman, and he went away to make war with the remnant of her seed, those who keep the commandments of God and have the testimony of Jesus." In this last stage, the dragon attacks the remnant of the woman's seed, which are the faithful people who follow Jesus at the end of time.

Remember, this section of the book is all about the dragon's war against the saints. Chapter 12, verse 17, introduces the final phase of that war. The following graphic presents a summary of chapters 12, 13, and 14. It gives more details there than I will explore in this presentation, but you may find them interesting and helpful.

The dragon's attack on the remnant in chapter 12, verse 17, gives us a nutshell picture of the final battle of earth's history. That battle is pictured more fully in chapters 13 and 14. Chapter 13 unpacks in detail what the dragon

Stage 3: The Dragon and the Remnant

Revelation 12	Revelation 13	Revelation 14
	The Dragon's War	The Remnant's Response

Revelation 12	Revelation 13	Revelation 14
vv. 1–6 Dragon attacks the male child	vv. 1–10 The rise and character of the sea beast	vv. 1–5 The remnant described
vv. 7–9 War in heaven Song of victory	vv. 11, 12 The land beast	vv. 6–12 The remnants' message
vv. 13–16 Dragon attacks the woman	vv. 13–18 The final attack on God's people	v. 13 Blessing
v. 17 Dragon attacks the remnant		vv. 14–20 The two harvests (the Second Coming)

does to destroy the remnant, the people of God. And chapter 14 shows the tables being turned on him. There you see the remnant's response to the dragon's attack.

Chapter 13, verse 1, pictures the dragon going to the

beach. He does so because he's been fighting God for thousands of years, and he's lost every previous battle. He's about to begin his final attack, so he goes to the beach to get some help. There he meets a beast that comes up out of the sea: "And I saw a beast coming up out of the sea, having ten horns and seven heads, and upon his horns ten royal crowns, and upon his heads the names of blasphemy." A second beast arises too. Chapter 13, verse 11, says, "I saw another beast, this one coming up out of the earth. He had two horns like a lamb and spoke like a dragon."

So you have the dragon standing on the beach, and while he's standing there, a beast comes up from the sea and another beast comes up from the earth and the two join him—three opponents of God joining forces. In the book of Revelation, God is often referred to in terms of Three: the Father, the Son, and the Holy Spirit. Christians call Them the Holy Trinity. In Chapter 13, there are echoes of the Father, Son, and Holy Spirit in the dragon, the sea beast, and the land beast. Like the Father, the dragon is the head of the group, the one who gives his authority to the sea beast.

The sea beast is actually a counterfeit of Jesus Christ. It looks like the dragon—just as Jesus mirrors the Father. He said, in fact, "Anyone who has seen me has seen the

Father" (John 14:9, NIV). The sea beast has a death and a resurrection, just like Jesus. It also has a ministry that lasts about three and a half years. So in many ways the sea beast is actually a counterfeit of Jesus Christ.

And the land beast is a counterfeit of the Holy Spirit. He speaks on behalf of the sea beast, like the Holy Spirit, who speaks on behalf of Christ. The land beast brings fire down from heaven, just as the Holy Spirit brought fire down on the Day of Pentecost. The land beast also gives breath to the image of the beast and brings it to life. There's a spiritual, "Holy Spirit" kind of atmosphere around this land beast.

Thus, these three creatures are actually a counterfeit trinity. They're deliberately counterfeiting the truth of God.

As we can see, then, in the last days of earth's history, truth and error will be very close together. It will be very hard to tell them apart. How can we distinguish them at the end of time? The best way is to stay close to the Word of God—to study the Bible, and particularly, the book of Revelation.

The two beasts of Revelation 13 each have a history. Each goes through two stages of activity. They come up as mature creatures—which reveals that they've already been active. The chapter moves them from past tenses

The Dragon and His Allies—The Time of Revelation 13

| | Revelation 13:1–7, 11 | Revelation 13:12–16 | Revelation 13:8,12–17 |
	PAST	PRESENT	FUTURE
Rev. 13:1–10	• Rise of the sea beast • Forty-two months • Death & resurrection • Persecution of saints	Works through land beast	Everyone will worship the beast
Rev. 13:11–18	• Rise of the land beast • Looks like lamb • Speaks like dragon	• Exercises authority of the sea beast • Performs great signs • Deceives those who live on the earth	• Makes an image • Causes the image to speak • Forces all to worship • Forces all to receive mark

that identify the beasts and their actions before the end to present and future tenses, which identify their actions in the final battle.

The sea beast seems to have a longer history because there are seven verses in the past tense to describe its past activity (13:1–7), while there's just one verse in the past tense to describe the land beast's previous activity (13:11). So when the dragon gains these beasts as allies in the final battle, they aren't new entities. They already have a history—a fact that is helpful in identifying them.

When you do advanced studies in the book of Revelation, you'll be interested to study some of that history. You'll want to learn who these beasts might be and discover where they came from. Then you'll be better able to recognize events as they occur in the final battle of earth's history.

The remnant

We'll turn our focus now to chapter 14 and its description of the "remnant." A lot of the book of Revelation focuses on the dark forces of the world, so it's nice to know that it also has a very strong positive message about what God can do for people who are faithful to Him. Those who study this book, those who are faithful to God, will find that God has a plan for the final battle, and a very special role for His people—the remnant—to play. In this brief outline of Revelation, we'll cover just a small portion of what that role involves.

We begin our look at the remnant with chapter 12, verse 17, again. "And the dragon was angry with the woman, and he went away to make war with the *remnant* of her seed, those who keep the commandments of God and have the testimony of Jesus" (emphasis added).

What can we deduce about this remnant, this final people of God?

First of all, we know they keep the commandments of God. In other words, they offer God full, willing obedience.

I think most human beings are willing to obey God up

to a point. But there does seem to come a point when we start to argue with God just a little bit: "Well, that may make sense for some people, but it isn't for me at this stage in my life." However, at the end of time, God's people won't be selectively faithful. They'll offer complete obedience to God. And the fact that the text highlights the remnant's keeping of the commandments indicates that other people are in some way refusing to obey one or more of God's commandments.

The remnant also have "the testimony of Jesus." Though much can be said about what that means, for now I'll just say that the testimony of Jesus is another way of talking about the prophetic gift. The gift of prophecy will be a part of what the remnant is all about at the end of time.

Chapter 14 unpacks in detail the remnant's side of the battle. In that chapter, God gives a number of characteristics of this special group. Chapter 14, verse 1, says, "And I saw, and behold, the Lamb already standing on Mount Zion, and with Him are 144,000 having His name and the name of His Father written on their foreheads." One characteristic of the remnant, then, is that they have the name of the Lamb and the name of His Father written on their foreheads.

The ancient Hebrews gave their children names that

would express their character. For example, when Jacob and his twin brother, Esau, were being born, Jacob was hanging on to Esau's heel as if he were trying to pull Esau back into the womb so he could be born first. So they named him *Jacob,* "supplanter," because he was trying to supplant his brother as firstborn.

God's people, the remnant—those who have His name and the name of Jesus, the Lamb, "written in their foreheads"—will have characters like that of God and Jesus. The divine character will be imprinted in their minds and in their hearts.

The text continues, "These follow the Lamb wherever He goes" (verse 4). Those who comprise the remnant will be in relationship with Jesus Christ. "They have been redeemed from among men as firstfruits to God and to the Lamb. And no lie was found in their mouths, they are blameless" (verses 4, 5). In other words, they are authentic. They don't lie. They don't try to deceive. They're honest and open, willing to look at the evidence, willing to treat people fairly, and so forth. The remnant will have all the character qualities we see here. Don't you want to be one of them?

Verses 6 and 7 tell us what the remnant will do: "And I saw another angel flying in midheaven, having the everlasting gospel to preach to those who live on the earth, to every nation, tribe, language, and people. Saying with a loud voice, 'Fear God and give glory to Him, because the hour of His judgment has come, and worship Him who made the heaven, and the earth, and the sea, and the fountains of water.' "

So the remnant will bring to the world a message about God's judgment. They will say that a time of judgment has come.

Next we come to the verse that is at the center of the center of the center of the book of Revelation. It calls people to "worship Him who made the heaven, and the earth, and the sea, and the fountains of water." This is a call to worship the God of creation, the God of the Sabbath, because what we have here is an allusion to Exodus 20:11, the fourth commandment, which recalls the Creation. God's last-day people will emphasize His creative power, and they will emphasize the keeping of all God's commandments, including the one about the Sabbath.

There's more. Revelation 14:12 says of the remnant, "Here is the patience of the saints, those who keep the commandments of God and the faith of Jesus." Once again there is emphasis on the obedience of the remnant, the obedience of the saints. They will be faithful to God not just when it's convenient but under all circumstances and to the fullest extent of what they understand. They will also exhibit "the faith of Jesus." In other words, they will keep their focus on Jesus. What He did on the cross will be crucial to them.

Whenever people talk about obedience, the fear of legalism arises. That's particularly true when the conversation includes keeping the Sabbath. People begin to worry that obedience is some kind of legalism. It isn't. The gospel isn't about legalism. The gospel isn't about what we do; it's about what God has done for us.

Why bring up obedience then? What does it have to do with the gospel?

Simply this: the best response we can make to God for His mighty acts on our behalf for us is to be like Him, to follow Him, to do what Jesus did. When we keep the commandments, we're following in His footsteps. We are doing what He would do in our place. We are obeying, not in order to be saved but because of the salvation He has already given us.

If somebody gave you an enormous gift, wouldn't you want to express your appreciation by doing whatever they asked? Wouldn't you want to be their friend to honor their incredible generosity? Of course. The gift creates a natural response. So obedience to Jesus Christ is the natural response to the gospel.

The following graphic summarizes what Revelation

says about what the remnant believe and teach. The items listed are drawn from chapters 10–14 and include things I haven't mentioned in this book.

Twelve Characteristics of the Remnant

Jesus	The gospel
Daniel and Revelation	Authenticity
The heavenly sanctuary	Relationship
Obedience	Sabbath
Prophetic guidance	Creation
Character of God and Christ	Judgment

First of all, there is the gospel, which we saw in chapters 10, 12, and 14. The Cross and the gospel of Jesus Christ are always in the background of Revelation. The remnant won't be a legalistic people. We note also that the books of Daniel and Revelation will be an important part of the remnant's message. Many followers of Jesus say these books are full of mystery and aren't really important. But the things we have covered here suggest that Daniel and Revelation *are* an important part of what the end-time remnant studies and teaches.

Chapter 11 contains a message about the heavenly sanctuary. So we can conclude that what the Bible teaches about the sanctuary in heaven will also be a component of the remnant message. And so, as we have seen, will obedience. Other characteristics of the remnant include prophetic guidance, possessing the character God and of Jesus Christ, authenticity, a message about the judgment, Sabbath, Creation, and a personal relationship with Jesus.

Chapter 10 tells us that the major focus of chapters 10 through 14 is on the time of the end, the last major period of earth's history. This is the period that follows the close of Daniel's time prophecies. During this period the gospel will be preached to the world and the characteristics of the remnant will influence that proclamation. They are all outlined in Revelation as part of the end-time gospel.

Judaism, Islam, and Christianity

As I close this chapter, I want to show you something exciting. Since September 11, 2001, the tension between Christianity, Islam, and Judaism has been growing. Each religion claims to be about the worship of the One True God, and each has borne witness to aspects of God's character.

But whenever people are at odds, they tend to pull

away from the things their opponents emphasize because they don't want to look like the "enemy." In the process they give up ideas that God may have wanted them to keep. When the Jews and Christians separated in the first century, it was almost as if they took the truth of God that they had shared and divided it. They both lost some important things in this process. Then Muhammad came along and tried, I believe, to bring them back to what they had lost. But this attempt failed, and the three faiths hardened against each other.

Whenever anyone holds different beliefs than we do, it is easy to say, "If I'm right, then you must be wrong." That's a dangerous conclusion, because when we're pointing an accusatory finger at everyone else, we're likely to miss what God may want to teach us through them— even in the midst of ideas that have many flaws.

It is easy to compare the best of our religion with the worst of another's religion and come away feeling good about ourselves. But that's neither fair nor constructive. What would happen if we saw the best in each other's faiths? We might be surprised.

What are the best, most positive contributions each of these monotheistic faiths have made to the world? And what unique, core aspects of each of these faiths have the other two rejected? For Christianity, it's been the gospel, grace, and Jesus. Judaism and Islam have elements of grace, but not the fullness that the gospel presents. The core values of Judaism that for the most part the other two reject are law, obedience, and Sabbath. And Islam emphasizes submission, judgment, and eschatology. Much of Christianity and Judaism have shied away from these latter themes in part because Muslims proclaim and practice them.

The core values of these three religions have become symbols of division. But when we look at them carefully,

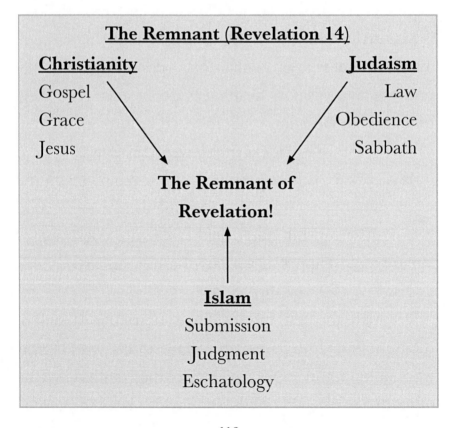

we begin to discover that the remnant of Revelation expresses all of them. (See the chart on page 113.) Evidently, it is God's purpose that in the end of time, there will be a body of people who will be faithful to the book of Revelation in its fullness. And out of that faithfulness will come a structure of belief, a structure of life practice that will be equally attractive to believers in all the great faiths on this earth. Nineteen hundred years ago, God designed a message that would be uniquely fitted to the time in which we live. So, God's remnant people will have a message not just for Christians, but also for Jews, for Muslims, for Buddhists, and for Hindus—for all people. The final remnant will draw all those who are faithful to God into one people to meet Jesus when He comes. This is only the beginning of a glimpse. But Revelation tells me that the best days for God's faithful people are still ahead.

Seven Keys · *Part Four*

Chapter Seven

The Wrath of God

WE BEGIN this chapter with Revelation 16:12. This verse describes the sixth plague, which is part of a series of seven plagues or seven disasters that the pouring out of the seven bowls will trigger. The sixth plague launches the battle of *Armageddon*— a term mentioned only once in the Bible, in verse 16 of chapter 16. Verse 12 says, "The sixth angel poured out his bowl on the great river Euphrates, and its water was dried up in order that the way of the kings from the rising of the sun might be prepared."

Notice three specific elements in this verse: the "great river Euphrates," the water drying up, and "the kings from the rising of the sun." We must identify these three elements if we're going to understand this text. Just what is this river, and how does it function in this prophecy? Is it the actual river that flows through Iraq today? Is it a symbol of the territory through which the Euphrates passes? Does it have something to do with the Iraq War?

What is meant by the drying up of the river Euphrates? And who are these kings from the rising of the sun?

In the first chapter of this book, we looked at a variety of methods for understanding Revelation. We'll apply three of those methods to help us understand this text and the context of the verse in question, its Old Testament allusions, and what other parts of the New Testament have to say about the matter.

The drying up of the Euphrates

Chapter 17, verse 1, says, "One of the seven angels who had the seven bowls came and spoke with me. . . ." This tells us that chapter 17 is about one of the seven bowls of chapter 16. Not all seven—chapter 17 focuses on just one.

How can we tell which of the seven bowls is in view here? One clue in chapter 17, verse 1, is that the vision has something to do with water. The angel tells John, "Come, I will show you the judgment of the great prostitute who sits on many waters."

Which of the seven bowls has to do with water? The second bowl falls on the sea, the third falls on the rivers and springs, and the sixth falls on the Euphrates River, so these three are the best candidates. Chapter 17, verse 1, uses the phrase "many waters." That phrase comes from the Old Testament, from Jeremiah 51:13. There it says that the citizens of Babylon live by "many waters."

What are the "many waters" of Babylon? The river Euphrates flowed right through the middle of Babylon, dividing that city into two roughly equal parts. Because Babylon was out in the desert, these were the only waters that Babylon lived by. So when the angel said, "I will show you the judgment of the great prostitute who sits on many waters," the angel was most likely referring to the Euphrates River.

That possibility is confirmed when we discover the name of the great prostitute in this text. Chapter 17, verse 5, says about her: "A name was written on her forehead, Mystery, Babylon the Great, the mother of prostitutes and of the abominations of the earth." So, in this instance the book of Revelation explains itself. If the prostitute of chapter 17 is Babylon, then the many waters of chapter 17 must be the Euphrates River. That means chapter 17 focuses on the sixth bowl plague, the one that fell on the Euphrates River.

Later on in chapter 17, the author of Revelation unpacks the meaning of the Euphrates River. We find that in verse 15: "[The angel] said to me, 'The waters which you saw, where the prostitute sits are peoples and crowds and nations and languages.' "

What are the waters which John saw? The Euphrates River.

What does the Euphrates River mean? "Peoples and crowds and nations and languages"—in other words, the secular, political powers of the world.

So, the Euphrates River is a symbol. It represents worldwide political power. It represents the nations of the world, their armies, their wealth, and so forth.

If that is so, what does the drying up of the waters of the Euphrates mean? In what way can the political powers of the world "dry up"?

To answer that question, we must go back to the Old Testament. The drying up of the great river Euphrates is a theme in passages like Jeremiah 50; 51; Isaiah 44–47; and Daniel 5. It's not my intention to go through these passages in detail, but I'll give you a glimpse of what they say.

The fall of Babylon

Jeremiah 50 describes the fall of ancient Babylon—and that event becomes the model Revelation uses to describe the end-time battle. Verses 33 and 34 tell us why Babylon was to be destroyed:

This is what the LORD Almighty says:

"The people of Israel are oppressed,
    and the people of Judah as well.
All their captors hold them fast,
    refusing to let them go.

"Yet their Redeemer is strong;
    the LORD Almighty is his name.
He will vigorously defend their cause
    so that he may bring rest to their land,
    but unrest to those who live in Babylon"
      (Jeremiah 50:33, 34, NIV).

Why did ancient Babylon come to an end? Because the Babylonians were persecuting the people of God. Verses 35 and 36 continue the fall-of-Babylon theme:

"A sword against the Babylonians!"
    declares the LORD,
"against those who live in Babylon
    and against her officials and wise men!
A sword against her false prophets!
    They will become fools.
A sword against her warriors!
    They will be filled with terror" (NIV).

So this text speaks of officials, wise men, prophets, and warriors. Who are these people? They're the people who made Babylon strong—her thinkers, her administrators, her religious leaders, her prophets, her warriors, her armies. Babylon is strong because her people are strong, because they are wise, because they are rich.

Verse 37 continues the theme,

"A sword against her horses and chariots
    and all the foreigners and her ranks!
    They will become women.
A sword against her treasures!
    They will be plundered" (NIV).

Once again we're looking at the resources of Babylon: her armies, her hired allies, her treasures. Babylon has lots of money, so she can hire soldiers, she can buy allies, and so forth. All of these verses are listing the strengths of Babylon, which are the basis of her power as a nation.

Now, look at verse 38:

"A drought on her waters.
    They will dry up.
For it is a land of idols,
    idols that will go mad with terror" (NIV).

The waters of Babylon—meaning the Euphrates River—
are one of Babylon's resources. They're part of what pro-
tects Babylon. They function like a moat that goes both
through and around the city. The drying up of the Euphrates, then, is a symbol of Babylon losing her defenses. God
destroys Babylon by taking away her support system. The
river Euphrates represents all the resources of Babylon.
Take them away, and Babylon falls.

This is brought out again in Isaiah 44:24, 27, 28:

I am the LORD . . .
who says to the watery deep, "Be dry,
    and I will dry up your streams,"
who says of Cyrus, "He is my shepherd
    and will accomplish all that I please;
    he will say of Jerusalem, 'Let it be rebuilt,'
    and of the temple, 'Let its foundations be laid' "
        (NIV).

Babylon stood in what is now Iraq, and Persia was to
its east, in what is now Iran. So, Cyrus, the Persian king,
brings his army from Persia, from the east, surrounds
Babylon, and tries to find a way to conquer it. Babylon
was a powerful city with very high walls. It was very difficult to attack. But Cyrus came up with a brilliant idea.

He said to his men, "Let's divert the Euphrates into a gigantic depression. Then, by marching down the riverbed we can get past the walls of the city and conquer it."

That's what happened. Cyrus's men marched along the riverbed into the center of Babylon. There they discovered that inner walls ran along the banks of the river too. But the night of their attack, the king of Babylon was throwing a big party, and the guards who watched the gates along the river got drunk. They didn't notice that the waters of the river were going down, and worse yet, they left the internal river gates open. So, Cyrus's army was able to march right into the city. As a result of Cyrus's conquest of Babylon, the people of God held captive

The Fall of Babylon

Old Testament	New Testament
Cyrus	End-time Cyrus
Euphrates	End-time Euphrates
Babylon	End-time Babylon
Israel	End-time Israel
Jerusalem	New Jerusalem

there were released and allowed to return to Judah and to rebuild their home city, Jerusalem.

To summarize, then, Cyrus, the king from the east, dries up the Euphrates River, conquers Babylon, delivers the people of God, and then directs the rebuilding of Jerusalem. This background story lies between the lines of the last third of the book of Revelation, chapters 15 through 22. There is an end-time Cyrus (and Darius, a co-ruler)—kings from the east—who dry up the end-time Euphrates (16:12) to conquer end-time Babylon (17; 18). They deliver end-time Israel (19; 20) and build a New Jerusalem (21; 22).

If we don't notice this fall-of-Babylon background, if we don't pay attention to the Old Testament, we'll completely miss what is going on in Revelation 16 and 17. It is only by paying deep and detailed attention to the Old Testament that we can fully understand the book of Revelation. The more we understand the Bible as a whole, the clearer the book of Revelation becomes.

Kings from the rising of the sun

Let's go back to chapter 16, verse 12: "The sixth angel poured out his bowl on the great river Euphrates, and its water was dried up in order that the way of the kings from the rising of the sun might be prepared." It is the third point that we're interested in now. Who are these kings from the rising of the sun?

This time the answer is found in the New Testament. Elsewhere, it uses the word *sunrise* in two different ways. It uses *sunrise* as a directional term—simply another way of saying "east." The Greeks would say, "I was looking toward sunrise, I was traveling toward sunrise," and everyone listening realized that means the direction east. So, for example, the wise men who visited the Baby Jesus came from the "sunrise," that is, they came from the east.

Second, this term is used in the New Testament in relation to Jesus Christ. For example, in Luke 1:78, Zechariah sings a song celebrating the birth of John the Baptist in which he refers to Jesus as the "rising sun who will come to us from heaven" (NIV). This translation is based on the same word as that which John used in Revelation 16. In Matthew 24:27, Jesus said His second coming would be like lightning that comes from the "sunrise"—from the east—and shines to the west. So this term *sunrise* is used in the New Testament as a reference to Jesus before His birth and as a reference to His second coming.

Revelation 7:2 is another text that uses the same word: "And I saw another angel ascending from the rising of the sun, having the seal of the living God." Here, again, divine action proceeds from the east. So throughout the

New Testament, the Greek word translated "sunrise" can simply mean a direction or it can be a reference to Jesus Christ and the work of God.

What does sunrise mean in chapter 16, verse 12? Do you remember the background story—that Cyrus and Darius came from the east? The kings from the east came and dried up the river Euphrates. They conquered Babylon, delivered Israel, and rebuilt Jerusalem. That's the background story.

In the main story, then, the kings from the sunrise represent a positive entity, not a negative one. In the New Testament, "east" is never negative. That means the coming of the kings from the sunrise brings about the fall of Babylon and the deliverance of God's people in the battle of Armageddon. The "kings from the rising of the sun" are a positive reference; they aren't some subgroup of the political powers of the world.

Let's go one step further. The kings from the rising of the sun are another way of describing Jesus and those faithful to Him. This becomes clear in the light of chapter 17, verse 14. Speaking of the final battle of Armageddon, this verse says, "These will make war with the Lamb, but the Lamb will overcome them, because He is Lord of lords and King of kings—and those with Him are called and chosen and faithful."

Who makes war against the forces of evil? The Lamb and those who are with Him. Who are with Him? His called, chosen, and faithful followers. The kings from the east—plural—are actually the faithful people of God in association with Jesus Christ.

Can the people of God be called kings?

Look back at chapter 1, verses 5, 6: "To the One who loves us, and has freed us from our sins by His blood, and has made us a kingdom, priests before God, even His Father." There we see the people of God, those who follow Jesus, called "a kingdom and priests."

In chapter 17, verse 14, Jesus is called "Lord of lords and King of kings." He's not just a King, He's an Emperor. And who are the kings under Him? His faithful people. The "kings of the east" refers to the final generation of the saints, those who earlier in the book have been called the remnant.

The battle of Armageddon

Some readers may be saying, "Wait a minute. Are you telling me the battle of Armageddon is a spiritual battle? I thought it's about tanks and planes and bombs and terrorists and all that kind of stuff."

Chapter 16, verse 14, speaks of earth's final battle. It

says, "[The frogs] are the spirits of demons, doing signs, which go out to the kings of the whole inhabited world to gather them for *the battle of the great day of God Almighty*" (emphasis added). Verse 16 also picks up on this theme: "And he gathered them to the place that in Hebrew is called Har-Magedon."

There it is—that *Armageddon* word! There we see the battle. Does it seem to be political? Does it seem to be military? It certainly does on the surface. The language there is the language of a final, decisive military battle. So, verses 14 and 16 fit together beautifully—but then the author complicates things by inserting verse 15 into the middle of this beautiful fit: "Behold, I come as a thief! Blessed is the one who stays awake and hangs on to his garments, in order that he might not walk naked and they see his shame."

What does verse 15 have to do with Armageddon? How does what it says fit into a military battle?

The statement in verse 15 echoes a number of texts in the New Testament that talk about *spiritual* preparation for the second coming of Jesus. The Gospels and Paul's letters contain statements that say in effect, "The Day of the Lord will come like a thief, so you'd better stay awake. You'd better hang on to your clothes. You'd better not get drunk." And the message to Laodicea in Revelation 3 talks about nakedness and shameful exposure. These are all reminders to prepare spiritually for the return of Jesus.

So, what is the point of chapter 16, verse 15? In the middle of the main text about the battle of Armageddon there is a reference to spiritual preparation for the coming of Jesus. The book of Revelation isn't primarily concerned about political and military events; it's primarily concerned with how such events affect the people of God.

As we consider the role of those saints in the final battle, I want to show you the clearest indication of how military language is used in the New Testament. Look at 2 Corinthians 10:3, 4: "For though we live in the world, we do not wage war as the world does. The weapons we fight with are not the weapons of the world. On the contrary, they have divine power to demolish strongholds" (NIV).

Now there's military language. This passage talks about war, about weapons—"the weapons of the world." It talks about strongholds—military defensive positions. What is this all about? What kind of battle is this New Testament passage talking about?

Look at verse 5. "We demolish arguments and every pretension that sets itself up against the knowledge of God, and we take captive every thought to make it obedient to Christ" (NIV). What kind of battle is this?

The battle of Armageddon is in fact a battle for the

mind. What counts at the end of time is the proclamation of the gospel, God's final appeal to the whole world. That's what the battle of Armageddon is all about. The language is military. The names and the concepts are drawn from Old Testament passages about literal battles. But the content of this battle is in harmony with the New Testament.

In Revelation, Israel represents the faithful church of God. Cyrus represents Christ. Babylon and the Euphrates represent not so much military and political powers as the opponents of Christ and of the people who are faithful to Him at the end of time. In other words, Armageddon isn't primarily a military or political battle. It's a battle for the mind. It's a battle for the thoughts. It's a battle for the hearts of the people of this earth. It's primarily a spiritual battle.

End-time confederacies

The book of Revelation outlines three great worldwide confederacies that will exist at the end of time. These three confederacies are the saints; the secular, political powers; and the religious powers of the world.

Earlier in this chapter we noted Revelation's picture of the prostitute named Babylon who "sits" on the Euphrates

River. Babylon represents end-time counterfeit religion. Yes, there will be religion in the end time that is not faithful to God. That will be the powerful religion, the popular religion, the institutional religion. This confederacy of religion is symbolized in Revelation by the great city, the great prostitute, and the unholy trinity.

The confederacy of the saints, on the other hand, represents all who are faithful to God at the end. This confederacy is given a variety of symbols and names, such as the remnant, the 144,000, the great multitude, the called and chosen, and the kings from the east. A minority, they will be known by their faithfulness, not by their allegiance to a specific popular religion.

I don't see this as an ecumenical movement in which various religions unite into one giant institution. Whenever that's been tried in the course of history, it has resulted in people being forced to act against their conscience. Instead, I see the confederacy of the saints as a voluntary fellowship of kindred spirits who recognize each others' faithfulness to the One True God. They may come from every tribe, every language, every people, and every religious background, but they unite on the common ground of faithfulness to Jesus and to His end-time message.

In addition, there will be a third major confederacy at the end. That will be a confederacy of military, economic, and political power, symbolized by the Euphrates River, by the kings of the world, by the many waters, by the earth dwellers, the ten horns, and more. There are many symbols for political power in Revelation.

Revelation's Terms for the Three Major End-time Confederacies

The Saints	Secular Forces	Religious Forces
Remnant	Euphrates	Babylon
144,000	Kings of the world	The great city
The great crowd	Many waters	The great prostitute
The watchful	Earth dwellers	The unholy trinity
The clothed	The beast	The woman
The called	The ten horns	
The chosen	The cities of the nations	
The faithful	The seven mountains	
	The seven kings	

When these three major confederacies form in the last days of earth's history, the final events move rapidly. "These [the ten horns, acting in behalf of the beast and the prostitute] will make war with the Lamb, but the Lamb will overcome them, because He is Lord of lords and King of kings—and those with Him are called and chosen and faithful" (Revelation 17:14). This text portrays the political powers of the world serving the confederacy of false religion by attempting to destroy the faithful people of God—and failing because of the Lamb's intervention.

Notice what happens when the nations realize they have failed, "The ten horns and the beast you saw, these will come to hate the prostitute" (17:16). The worldwide confederacy of nations will turn Babylon against their religious masters. "And she will be made desolate and naked and they will eat her flesh and burn her up with fire. For God has placed it in their hearts to do His purpose, and to be of one purpose themselves, and to give their domain and power to the beast until the words of God are brought to completion" (verses 16, 17).

In other words, Revelation predicts that, at the end of time, the forces in opposition to God will fail to accomplish their purpose of destroying the remnant because God is in control. God is moving events and bringing about His will. Then they will end up fighting each other.

Here's the amazing thing. God oversees all the final events of earth's history. No matter how bad things get, nothing is out of God's control. He permits nothing that would ultimately, eternally, hurt His people.

The order of end-time events

So, at this point we can list the end-time events in the book of Revelation in the approximate order in which they will occur:

1. The gospel goes to the world, giving everyone the opportunity of responding to it.
2. A counterfeit gospel arises (represented by the deception of the unholy trinity and by the three frogs that go out to the kings of the world).
3. The nations of the world establish some form of worldwide political unity.

These three developments result in three great end-time confederacies. Will worldwide political unity be established first? Or the gospel confederacy—or the counterfeit? That's not entirely clear. But it is clear that eventually these three will exist simultaneously.

4. The world will be brought to one last time of decision, one last opportunity either to follow Jesus or to resist His rulership.
5. At the time of this final proclamation of the gospel, the religious and political authorities of the world will unite. For the only time in history, all the political

powers and all the religious powers of the earth will have a single purpose: to destroy the work of God.

6. The saints—known also as the remnant and the 144,000—will be singled out for destruction. In a limited sense, this has already happened many times. In the Middle Ages, the faithful people of God experienced tremendous persecution. In more recent times, God's people have suffered terribly in many places, such as in communist lands. But at the end of time, there will be a *universal* attempt to destroy the faithful people of God.

7. Probation will close. There will be no more opportunity to receive the gospel.

8. The political and religious powers of this world will attack the saints, attempting to destroy them all.

9. Christ will intervene, defeating the attack of the world's political and religious powers.

10. The nations, the political powers of the earth, furious at having been deceived by the religious powers, will turn on them and destroy them.

11. Christ's second advent will take place, and He will destroy the political powers that sought to harm the people of God.

12. Finally, Christ will gather the saints to be with Him throughout eternity.

Chapter Eight

The Millennium

THE TEACHING about the millennium, the thousand-year period described in Revelation 20, has long been one of the most controversial portions of the book. Let's see what we can learn about it.

Some interesting characters enter the story in the chapters we just covered. The dragon makes his first appearance in chapter 12, the sea beast and earth beast—also known as the false prophet—show up in chapter 13, and Babylon is named for the first time in chapter 14. So each of these four characters enters the story in chapters 12 through 14.

I find it interesting—and helpful to our understanding of Revelation—that these characters leave the story in the reverse order from that in which they entered it. Babylon is destroyed first (chapter 18), then the false prophet and the sea beast (chapter 19), and finally the dragon (chapter 20).

The appearance and disappearance of these major

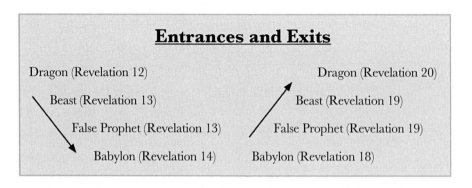

characters makes a continuous narrative of the story told in chapters 12 through 20.

Over the centuries, people have debated whether the millennium comes before or after the second coming of Jesus. But if Revelation 12 through 20 tells a continuous story, then the millennium comes at the end of that story rather than at its beginning or middle. That means the millennium isn't part of the Christian age (which runs from the Cross to the Second Coming), as some have suggested. It's at the very end. The millennium comes *after* the fall of Babylon, after the fall of the beast and the false prophet, at the time when God deals with the dragon— with Satan himself.

Take a look at chapter 20, verse 4: "And I saw thrones, and they sat on them, and judgment was given to them. And I saw the souls of those who had been beheaded because of the testimony of Jesus and the Word of God. These did not worship the beast or his image, neither did they receive the mark upon their foreheads or upon their hands." One thing about the timing of this judgment is clear: it occurs at the beginning of the millennium. Verse 4 says these "souls" came to life and *reigned a thousand years.*

Could the millennium have begun at the time of Jesus and His disciples, as some suggest? I don't think so. Verse 4 says of these "souls" that they didn't worship the beast or his image, nor receive his mark upon their foreheads or their hands. In other words, they successfully resisted the pressure exerted by the false trinity—pressure, persecution, that is associated with the end of the Christian era, with the time just before the second coming of Jesus. Their faithfulness through those times is what has qualified them to be seated on the thrones of judgment. To say it directly, the millennium follows the second coming of Jesus.

Some have suggested that the resurrection at the beginning of the millennium is a spiritual one; that it is about people coming to faith and being renewed spiritually. But the language of resurrection here is not spiritual language; it is literal, physical language. Verse 4 says, "I saw the souls of those who had been beheaded." Nowhere does the Bible speak of a spiritual beheading. That is a very physical act.

The passage says, "they came to life and reigned with Christ for a thousand years. . . . This is the first resurrection" (verses 4, 5). Elsewhere in the Bible, terms like "came to life" and "resurrection" never refer to spiritual resurrection from spiritual death. Scripture always uses them to speak of physical resurrection from physical death. And it is at the second coming of Jesus that His faithful followers are raised from the dead. Those who died in the conflict over the image of the beast and his mark (13:15–17) come up from their graves and reign with Christ for a thousand years.

The Bible doesn't wrap up the story of salvation at the Second Coming. It indicates that there's more God has to do beyond that event to finish the process. (See not only Revelation 20 but also 1 Corinthians 15 and Isaiah 24.) That work gets done during the millennium.

Where are the people of God during that time? Are they on the earth or in heaven? The only passage in the Bible that clearly addresses that issue is John 14:1–3. There Jesus says, "Do not let your hearts be troubled. You believe in God, believe also in Me. In My Father's house there are many rooms; if it were not so, I would have told you. I go to prepare a place for you, and if I go and I prepare a place for you, I will come again and I will receive you to Myself, in order that where I am, you may be also."

Jesus is now preparing a place in heaven for His people. He didn't say, "I will come again so I can be where you are." He said, "I will come again so you can be with Me where I am." He will take them to that place.

This text reminds me of ancient Hebrew weddings. The engagement took place at the house of the bride-to-be. Then the groom went back to his father's house, and there he prepared the place where the newlyweds would live. Meanwhile, the bride stayed at her father's house and prepared herself for the wedding. So, the groom prepared the house, and the bride prepared herself.

On the wedding day, the groom traveled from his father's house to the place where the bride lived, and he took her back to the place he had prepared at his father's house so they could marry and she could live with him. It was only after the wedding that the bride went to the home where they would live together.

This is the background story to John 14:1–3. It tells us that when Jesus comes, He doesn't come to be with His people. Rather, He comes to bring them home to where He lives—His Father's house. So the righteous aren't on earth during the thousand years of Revelation 20; instead, they're in heaven with Jesus.

What happens during the millennium?

What's happening on earth during the millennium?

Revelation 20:1–3 says, "I saw an angel coming down out of heaven, having the key of the Abyss and a great chain in his hand. And he seized the dragon, the ancient serpent, who is the devil and Satan, and bound him for a thousand years. [So Satan is "bound" during this time.] He threw him into the Abyss, locked it, and sealed it over him in order that he might not deceive the nations anymore until the thousand years were finished. After these things he must be released for a short time."

The passage says Satan is prevented from deceiving the nations anymore. What stops him? One possibility is that while people are still living on the earth, God denies Satan access to them. But there's another possibility. As we just saw, John 14 says that at the Second Coming, Christ takes the righteous from the earth to heaven with Him. And many New Testament texts indicate that the wicked are destroyed at the Second Coming. (See, for example, Matthew 25:46; 2 Thessalonians 1:6–10; 2:8, 9.) This suggests that Satan is "bound" in the sense that he's restricted to earth and there are no people alive here during the millennium. There's no one around for him to deceive.

Revelation 20:1–3 also says the devil will be locked up in "the Abyss" during those thousand years. The concept of the abyss appears frequently in the Bible. Genesis 1:2

says that before God worked on this earth at Creation, it was without shape and unfilled "and there was darkness over the abyss." In other words, Genesis 1 calls the unformed world He had spun into space earlier "the Abyss." It was a mess. It was like a junkyard.

The same language comes up again in Jeremiah 4:23–27: "I beheld the earth, and, lo it was without form, and void [terms used in Genesis 1 to describe the earth before Creation] . . . I beheld, and, lo, there was no man, and all the birds of the heavens were fled. I beheld, and, lo, the fruitful place was a wilderness, and all the cities thereof were broken down at the presence of the LORD, and by his fierce anger. For thus hath the LORD said, the whole land shall be desolate, yet will I not make a full end" (KJV).

In other words, at this time the earth is empty, desolate, broken down. The people are gone, the wicked have been destroyed, the righteous have gone to heaven, and Satan is bound to this earth. He can't deceive anyone.

To summarize the premillennial view, the one I believe is correct: Much of the book of Revelation is concerned with the period from the cross of Jesus Christ to the Second Coming, but in chapter 20, the focus moves to the millennium, which begins at the Second Coming. During this thousand-year period, the righteous are in heaven and the wicked are dead. So, Satan, bound to this earth, which is desolate, can't deceive anyone. At the end of the millennium, the New Jerusalem comes down from heaven, there is a final confrontation between God and Satan and the wicked. Then the wicked and Satan are forever destroyed, and God makes the earth and the universe clean again.

A time of judgment

Why does God go through this complicated process? Why doesn't He just clean things up at the Second Coming? What's the point of the millennium?

I believe the millennium is a time of judgment. It seems to me that in Scripture, judgment proceeds through five phases: First, judgment takes place at the Cross (Revelation 12:10–12). Second, the preaching of the gospel sparks a judgment. As the white horse goes out, people are judged by whether they accept or reject the gospel (6:1–8). Third, there's a judgment shortly before the second coming of Jesus. The final proclamation of the gospel includes the message "the hour of His judgment *has* come" (14:7, emphasis added; see also 18:4–8). Fourth, there's a phase of the judgment during the millennium. God gives His people the opportunity to process, to understand—to judge, if you will—what He has done and what they have gone through (20:4). Fifth, the final phase of judgment is the lake of fire, the ultimate destruction of sin (20:10–15).

I think this is a beautiful part of Revelation. God doesn't destroy the wicked permanently until they have gone through a whole series of judgments. These judgments allow every creature in every part of the universe to see and to testify that God has done right, that God has judged justly. At the Cross and in the preaching of the gospel, God built the case for His love and justice in the face of sin. From the Second Coming through the millennium, God proves the case. He proves it to the unfallen universe. He proves it to those whom He has saved, who will be in heaven with Him for a thousand years. And then, at the end of the thousand years, He proves His righteousness even to those who have opposed Him.

Why go to all that trouble—five whole phases of judgment? Because God wants everybody to see His justice clearly before the end. Revelation 15:3, 4, says,

"Great and marvelous are Your works,
    Lord God Almighty.
Righteous and true are Your ways,
    King of the nations.

Who will not fear You, O Lord,
    and glorify Your name,
For You alone are holy?
All nations will come
    and worship before You,
Because Your righteous acts have been brought into
      the open."

At the climax of all things, the whole universe declares that God is just, that He is fair, that He has done what is right. His righteousness has been revealed.

In Ezekiel 38:16, God says, "In days to come, O Gog, I will bring you against my land, so that the nations may know me when I show myself holy through you before their eyes" (NIV). In other words, God's acts of saving His people and even of destroying the wicked will be justified. God wants everyone to be fully convinced that He's been fair, truthful, and loving.

Many people today doubt God's justice. Revelation says that He will take all the time necessary to fully convince the whole universe that He is just. He will satisfy all doubts and answer all questions. It will be clear that everyone has been judged fairly whether or not they've served God. His decisions will be vindicated at the end. The wicked will demonstrate this because even when all doubts are satisfied and all questions answered, they will still reject God and those who serve Him: they will try to attack the city of God, the New Jerusalem (Revelation 20:9). It is obvious that the universe couldn't be safe if they and their rebellion are allowed to continue.

In the end, there will be only two sides. On one side is the Lion/Lamb, and on the other side, the evil one. It may not always be clear to us now which side is just and right, but in the full picture of the final judgment, Jesus Christ will be seen as truly righteous, truly fair, and truly just. And all those who are willing to receive Him will see how beautiful His character is. All those who trust God will reject sin, abuse, strife, and all the things that cause such misery on earth now. In the end, there will be a beautiful conclusion: a new heaven and a new earth.

Chapter Nine

The New Heaven and New Earth

WHAT WILL heaven be like? Will it really be worth what it takes to get there? Will someone who has a PhD really want to live there? Will a Hollywood actor, a farmer, a business person, a city dweller, a country dweller, really want to be in heaven? What will people do for eternity?

I believe God's people will play three roles throughout eternity. They'll be kings, priests, and scholars. In the ancient world, kings had the highest status in the political realm. And priests had the highest status in the religious realm. God has chosen His faithful people to be kings and priests. They'll join Him in ruling the universe (Revelation 3:21; 7:15–17). They'll be part of His government. They'll sit with Him on His throne. They'll also be active in leading worship (5:9–13). They'll hold positions of spiritual power and influence in the universe.

Perhaps the scholar part worries you. You say, "I never liked school." Well, school can be boring. Yet when we learn at our own pace, when we learn about things we're interest in, when our curiosity piques our attention, learning isn't a chore. In fact, it's a joyous experience. And there are so many things in the universe to learn. We'll spend an eternity learning and growing, and it will be a delight.

Those who have suffered the most can be trusted with the highest place. Our days of usefulness and service won't end in eternity—they'll increase. He who is faithful in little things will be put in charge of big things (Matthew 25:21).

Conclusion

Eight Lessons From Revelation

THE BOOK of Revelation is full of excitement, full of battles, full of abuse, full of horror, full of strange animals. What's the spiritual takeaway in all of this? I'd like to suggest eight lessons we can learn from Revelation.

First, it's all about the Cross. If you read the book of Revelation and think it's primarily about politics, primarily about battles and wars, you're not reading it correctly. You're not seeing the deeper significance of the symbols. In the end, it's the revelation of Jesus Christ. It's about the slain Lamb. It's about the One who shed His blood so we can live. It's the basis for real life.

People seek for life in so many ways that can't satisfy. We try to find it in material goods. We try to find it in achievement. We try to find it in relationships. But in the end, self-worth comes only from the One who can say, "You are worth so much to Me that I died for you." When the One who is worth the entire universe dies for us, that's incredible value. The Cross is the basis for life. It's the basis for joy, the basis for purpose. And it's the fundamental teaching of the book of Revelation.

Second, a major point of the book of Revelation is the role of obedience. While the gospel provides everything we need to be saved, the natural response of those who have experienced that salvation is to obey Jesus Christ in everything that He invites us to do, keeping all of His commandments. Alongside the gospel, Revelation rightly emphasizes obedience.

Third, Revelation is about living accountably. It's about living in the realization of impending judgment. Revelation proclaims that the hour of God's judgment has come. It proclaims that in the end we will be kings and priests. And that means if our roles in eternity are going to be important, we need to start training now. Developing our skills in leadership. Developing our spiritual sense, our ability to worship God, because in eternity we'll be leading in the rulership and worship of the universe. It's kind of nice to know, as Joseph knew, "God sees me and everything I do."

Fourth, Revelation unmasks evil. In a Hollywood world, it's easy to think that sin is attractive. To think that sin is delightful. But in reality, sin is a destroyer. It sucks the life out of us. It will destroy us in the end. The book of Revelation portrays sin in all its ugliness.

Fifth, Revelation teaches us the need to be discerning. A great deception is coming—the greatest the world has ever seen. In the last days, it will be difficult to distinguish between truth and falsehood.

Sixth, Revelation shows us that the discernment we will need is found in the Word of God. It is only by understanding the Word, by knowing it, that we'll be able to find safe ground on which to stand at the end of time.

Seventh, we learn from Revelation that at the end, God will have a people faithful to Him, though they may not be a popular people. They may not seem to have it all together. Those people will find in each other kindred spirits and support for their service to the true God.

And eighth, the final message of the book of Revelation is that God wins. Things frequently fall apart for us now. That's particularly true when we worry about the future. We don't know what's going to happen. We don't know if we're going to have enough money. We don't know if we're going to survive. We don't know a lot of things, but the book of Revelation is a prophecy. It tells us, "Whatever you go through, whatever you experience in this life, at the end of the ultimate story God wins. No matter how out of control things get, God will make it right in the end."

What better way to end than with the promises that in the end, the *very* end, God wins—and that we can have a wonderful part of that victory—promises guaranteed to us by "the blood of the Lamb" (Revelation 12:11)?